Picture Palace to Penny Plunge

David Cliffe was born at Macclesfield, Cheshire, in 1946, when there were five cinemas operating, all of which he remembers. He studied English language and medieval English literature at the University of Leeds, followed by a postgraduate diploma in librarianship. Then he set about looking for work. The public library in Reading was the first institution to say 'yes', and he was employed there for the whole of his career, in a variety of posts.

In 1978, he wrote *The Stranger in Reading: An Unofficial Guide*, published by Reading Libraries, followed by a second edition in 1980.

With the abolition in 1998 of Berkshire County Council, for whom he had been County Reference Librarian, Reading Borough Council took him back. In many ways, the post of Local Studies Manager was an ideal way of ending his career in paid employment.

In 2007, *Roots and Branches* (Two Rivers Press) was published to celebrate the centenary of the opening of Battle and Caversham Libraries in Reading.

In his retirement, David continues to work on a voluntary basis on the vast and extensive local studies collection at Reading Central Library, making more of it available online. He is currently chairman of both the Berkshire Local History Association and the History of Reading Society and has three books of Macclesfield history awaiting publication, the first of which, on street-names, is due to appear in 2017.

Also published by Two Rivers Press

The Shady Side of Town: Reading's Trees by Adrian Lawson and Geoff Sawers
Reading: The Place of the People of the Red One by Duncan Mackay
A Wild Plant Year by Christina Hart-Davies
The Veiled Vale by Mike White
Before and After by Edith Morley, edited by Barbara Morris
Silchester by Jenny Halstead & Michael Fulford
The Writing on the Wall by Peter Kruschwitz
Caught on Camera by Terry Allsop
Allen W. Seaby by Martin Andrews & Robert Gillmor
Reading Detectives by Kerry Renshaw
Fox Talbot & the Reading Establishment by Martin Andrews
All Change at Reading by Adam Sowan
An Artist's Year in the Harris Garden by Jenny Halstead
Caversham Court Gardens by Friends of Caversham Court Gardens
Believing in Reading by Adam Sowan
Bikes, Balls & Biscuitmen by Tim Crooks & Reading Museum
Bizarre Berkshire by Duncan Mackay
The Reading Quiz Book by Adam Sowan
Broad Street Chapel & the Origins of Dissent in Reading by Geoff Sawers
Reading: A Horse-Racing Town by Nigel Sutcliffe
Down by the River by Gillian Clark
A Much-maligned Town by Adam Sowan
The Holy Brook by Adam Sowan
A Thames Bestiary by Peter Hay and Geoff Sawers
Abattoirs Road to Zinzan Street by Adam Sowan

Picture Palace to Penny Plunge

Reading's Cinemas

David Cliffe

The History of Reading Society

First published in the UK in 2017 by Two Rivers Press
7 Denmark Road, Reading RG1 5PA
www.tworiverspress.com

© History of Reading Society 2017

First published by Two Rivers Press on behalf of the History of Reading Society.
All rights reserved. No part of this publication may be reproduced, stored in
or introduced into a retrieval system, or transmitted, in any form, or by any means
(electronic, mechanical, photocopying, recording or otherwise) without the prior
written permission of the committee of The History of Reading Society.
www.historyofreadingsociety.org.uk

The right of David Cliffe to be identified as the author of the work has been
asserted by him in accordance with the Copyright, Designs and Patents Act of 1988.

ISBN 978-1-909747-31-9

1 2 3 4 5 6 7 8 9

Two Rivers Press is represented in the UK by Inpress Ltd and distributed by NBNi.

Cover design and illustration by Nadja Guggi based on a photograph
of the Grand Cinema in Broad Street which is reproduced by courtesy
of the Cinema Treasures website.
Text design by Nadja Guggi and typeset in Bembo and Parisine

Printed and bound in Great Britain by Imprint Digital, Exeter

Acknowledgements
All photographs by courtesy of Reading Borough Libraries, except for
the following: p. 21, p. 25, p. 40, John Whitehead; p. 53, anonymous donor;
p. 68, p. 71, Cinema Treasures; p. 74, Historic England; p. 81, Adj Messelles.

Preface

The origins of this book go back many years. When I arrived in this town as a young man, there were five cinemas, and I went to all of them. I had a job in the Central Library in Blagrave Street, and my favourite part of it was the local studies collection. It was while serving the public at the local studies desk in the new library in Abbey Square that I had a visit from two rather giggly schoolgirls. They had been told that the big building at the bottom of Norcot Hill had been a cinema. Was this true? They seemed somewhat incredulous when I told them that yes, this had been the Rex Cinema. They asked me why it had closed, and I mentioned television. This was something completely new to them. As far as they were concerned, television had always been around. I was sorry that there wasn't very much printed literature that I could put into their hands, and certainly nothing with photographs of the Rex.

Then, in 2013, soon after retiring from paid work, I was asked by the Reading branch of the Berkshire Family History Society if I would give a talk on Reading theatres and cinemas. They wanted a 90-minute talk, and I said that there was too much material for a single talk; I would do theatres *or* cinemas. Since I already had a talk on Reading theatres up my sleeve, that would have been the easy option. But I wanted a challenge, I was interested in cinemas, and since I had the best part of a year in which to prepare, I decided to investigate the cinemas.

The short section on cinemas in Daphne Phillips's book *Reading Theatres, Cinemas and Other Entertainments* gave me a good start, but, as I soon discovered, there had been many more cinemas than are mentioned in her book.

After the talk, many people in the audience came forward with reminiscences, and I found myself being pressed to write up my notes as a book. When I repeated the talk at Battle Library in shortened form, there were again some interesting reminiscences, many of which have found their way into this book. The committee of the History of Reading Society said that they would publish the book if I would write it. I have to admit here that I was then (and still am) the chairman of the society, but it was obvious to me that the other committee members thought it should be done.

I have many people to thank for making this book possible. There are the people who shared reminiscences, and there is a gentleman who gave me the 1940s photograph of the Caversham Electric Theatre. The 1920 programme of the Vaudeville Cinema was borrowed from fellow committee member John Whitehead, and I'm also grateful to several organisations which have allowed me to use their illustrations: Historic England, Ken Roe and the Cinema Treasures website, and especially Reading Borough Libraries. I'm also indebted to the three people who have kindly helped me improve the text. Another fellow committee member, Sidney Gold, read it and corrected several errors, and he made some helpful suggestions. Charles Morris, an independent cinema proprietor, has put me right on several points, especially in the opening section on technical developments. And Katie Amos has given me help in finding information in online databases.

Even so, I am only too aware that I will have made errors here and there and may have failed to mention things that ought to have been mentioned. I would have liked to track down the account books of one or two of the early cinemas to see what their overheads were, and how profitable they were. There may be more and better photographs of the buildings that could have been used. In many cases I have had to rely on newspaper photographs from the 1920s and 30s, re-photographing them from the fragile bound volumes in the Central Library.

Maybe there will be the chance of an expanded, second edition. Please get in touch through the History of Reading Society website if you have information or photographs to contribute.

David Cliffe
Caversham, Reading, February 2017

Contents

Part 1: Technical developments

1 Optical illusion
1 The projection of images
2 Photography
3 Film
4 Electricity
4 Colour
5 Sound
7 3-D
7 Wide screens
8 I-MAX® cinemas
8 Digital projection

Part 2: Cinemas and performances

10 Travelling and temporary shows, 1897–1909
11 Cinema in theatres, 1907–
11 The Cinematograph Act, 1909
12 Adapted cinemas, 1909–
12 Purpose-built cinemas, 1911–
13 Numbers of cinemas and seats, 1909–2009
14 Prices of admission
15 Multiplexes, 1999–
16 Ownership of cinemas
18 Sunday opening
19 Censorship
20 Programmes
22 Children's programmes
24 Pianos, organs and orchestras
27 Queues, tickets, usherettes, refreshments and smoking
29 Closure and rebirth

Part 3: The places where films were shown

- 32 Travelling shows, 1897–1909
- 33 Reading Town Halls, Blagrave Street, 1904–
- 34 A.H. Bull's department store, 52–58 Broad Street, 1904
- 35 The Palace Theatre, Cheapside, 1907–
- 35 The Reading Picture Palace, 16 Cross Street, 1909
- 36 The King's Hall (later Bio-Picture Land and the Standard Electric Theatre), 84 King's Road, 1909–c.1915
- 38 The Vaudeville Electric Theatre (later the Gaumont), 47 Broad Street, 1909–1957
- 44 West's Picture Palace, 37 West Street, 1909–c.1916
- 47 The Royal County Theatre, 113 Friar Street, 1910–1937
- 47 The Electric Automatic Vaudeville, 27 Broad Street, 1910
- 49 The Empire Picture Theatre, Elm Park Road, c.1909–c.1930
- 50 The Caversham Electric Theatre (later the Glendale), Church Street, Caversham, 1911–1977
- 54 The Paragon Electric Theatre, 29 King's Road, 1911–1913
- 55 The Howard Electric Theatre, Hosier Street, 1911–c.1913
- 56 The Grand, 100–101 Broad Street, 1911–1922
- 58 The London Street Pavilion, 112 London Street, from 1920
- 58 The Tilehurst Cinema, 15 Victoria Road, Tilehurst, 1920–c.1929
- 59 The Central Cinema (later the ABC Central, the Cannon, and the MGM), Friar Street, 1921–1999
- 63 The Pavilion (later the Gaumont), Oxford Road, 1929–1979
- 66 The Granby (later the ABC Granby, and the ABC London Road), 1935–1982
- 70 The Savoy, Basingstoke Road, 1936–1961
- 72 The Odeon, Cheapside, 1937–1999
- 76 The Rex, Oxford Road, 1937–1958
- 79 The Regal, Church Street, Caversham, 1938–1958
- 81 Reading Film Theatre, The Palmer Building, University of Reading, Whiteknights Park, 1970–
- 82 Studios 1 and 2 (Studio 1 later became Studio X), London Street, 1972–1978

83 The Hexagon, 1977–
83 The Warner Village (later Vue), The Oracle, 1999–
85 The Forbury Hotel, 2004–
85 Outdoor cinema
85 St Martin's Precinct, Caversham – ?

Appendices

86 Films made in or near Reading
91 Actors and directors with Reading connections
97 Ownership of cinemas in Reading
99 Sources
102 Index

Part 1:
Technical developments

Optical illusion

The illusion by which the brain interprets a series of consecutive still images as a continuous moving image has long been known. Many a child will have had fun turning an old school exercise book into a 'flicker book' by drawing a series of match-stick men on the corners of the pages, each one slightly different from the last.

In Victorian times, optical toys using this principle were being produced. They were given 'Greek' names, such as zoetrope, phenakistoscope and panorama. In the early days of the BBC news documentary programme 'Panorama', it was in fact a zoetrope that was shown at the beginning: a shallow cylinder that could be spun on a stand. Around the curved side of the cylinder was a series of slots at regular intervals, and inside the cylinder was a series of images, between the slots. If you looked through the slots as the cylinder spun, you could see a moving picture of a man running, or a horse galloping.

The projection of images

Glass lenses had been in use since the Renaissance to make spectacles to correct defective eyesight. The camera obscura was used by artists to project images onto a flat surface where they could be traced by hand. Versions of glass lantern slides had been around since the days of candles and oil-lamps: images painted onto the glass were used as a novelty for amusement. Gradually, better sources of artificial light were invented, usually involving dangerous gases and chemicals: for example the argand lamp, a kind of oil lamp, in the 1790s;

lime-light in the 1820s; and the arc lamp in the 1860s. All of these got dangerously hot. Nevertheless, it was the carbon arc lamp which was used in cinema projectors for many years. Safer Xenon arc lamps came into use in the 1960s, but carbon arcs survived in some cinemas into the twentieth century.

In a magic lantern, the semblance of motion could be created using two or more slides that were jiggled against one another to give the impression of a moving arm or leg. When this was first done in the 1730s, people were amazed. Magic lanterns were used at séances, where people thought that they were seeing ghosts.

At fairgrounds, 'ghost shows' were popular at the end of the nineteenth century and the beginning of the twentieth. Many of them used Pepper's Ghost Equipment, involving a mirror, a gauze screen and a projector underneath the stage, with the audience in a darkened booth. As the actors performed their melodrama, the 'ghost' appeared to float through the air. Having the projector on wheels or having two projectors created even more magical effects, and audiences were suitably thrilled.

Photography

Before you could have cinema, you needed a light source, you needed photography, and you needed film. Early photographs, such as those produced in France by Louis Daguerre, were on metal plates and could not be copied. In the 1840s, W.H. Fox Talbot, who for a time had a studio in Reading, played a major role in photographing onto glass plates and producing negatives from which many positive copies could be made. They could be printed onto paper, or onto glass so that they could be projected using a magic lantern.

The long exposure time needed to take photographs precluded real-time movie photography, and as yet there was no flexible transparent film. There were devices called the zoopraxiscope and the praxinoscope, which could show glass slides in rapid succession to give the impression of motion, but the images had to be painted onto the glass.

Film

Celluloid photographic film was invented in the 1880s, and in 1894 the Lumière Brothers were the first to demonstrate moving pictures to the public, in France and in Britain. It would be only a few years before moving pictures were shown in Reading. The father of the brothers ran a factory in Lyon that made photographic equipment; that first film showed the workers leaving the factory. Strangely, the Lumières could not see the importance of what they had accomplished. They are reputed to have said (in French!), 'The cinema is an invention without any future'.

Others continued where they had left off, especially in France, where the Pathé brothers acquired the Lumières' patents, and a company founded by Leon Gaumont was producing films by 1896. Many of the films that were shown in Britain were made in France in the early days of cinema, but after the First World War, filmmakers in the United States were in the ascendancy.

Early cinema-goers found the experience totally magical, despite the jerkiness of the motion, the scratches on the film, and the frequent breaking of the film. In his reminiscences, W.E. Woodeson, a Reading local historian, remembered the early days at the King's Hall, when the house-lights went up every time the film broke, and people showed their displeasure.

By 1912, the quality of film was improving. Wilfred Owen, the First World War poet, was less than enthusiastic about a visit to the cinema in 1912, though he conceded that the 'impression of driving through an electric hail storm on a

Chinese-cracker is not now so easily got as of old.' This was in a letter to his mother dated 22 September, and the film was *Queen Bess*, starring Sarah Bernhardt, which was on at the Vaudeville in Reading. A copy of the programme for this film survives in the County Record Office at Reading. At the time Owen was staying at Dunsden Vicarage, acting as a pupil and unpaid lay assistant of the vicar. He found the limitations of the film frustrating: 'All very well', he wrote, 'but it is positively painful to me not to hear speech; more than the case of a deaf man at a proper Shakespeare play; for all the finer play of mouth, eye, fingers, and so on, is utterly imperceptible, and so are the slower motions of the limbs spoiled, and their majesty lost, in the convulsed, rattling-hustle of the Cinema'.

Another concern at this time was the possible deleterious effect of cinema-going on people's eyesight, much like the scare in the 1950s over watching too much television.

Electricity

Although the Electric Supply Company had started generating on an island in the River Kennet in the 1880s, some cinema owners preferred to generate their own. Perhaps they considered the public supply to be too unreliable. The Paragon in King's Road used a steam traction engine in the yard outside to drive a generator, while the Goad insurance plan of Reading for 1911 shows that across the road, a gas engine in a room beside the auditorium was driving a generator at the King's Hall.

Colour

Hand-tinted films were around from the earliest days of the cinema. In 1910, the Vaudeville showed a 'coloured' film, *Scenery in Norway*, where the camera was mounted on a train.

Its rival, West's Picture Palace, was showing *Pygmalion*, twice nightly at 7 and 9pm, 'beautifully coloured'. The coloured ink was applied by hand, sometimes using stencils.

When the Grand opened in 1911, they were advertising 'Kinemacolor – the only natural colour pictures in the world, as exhibited at the Scala Cinema, London, and by royal command. Exclusive to Reading and district'. The Kinemacolor process was invented by a Brighton man, Albert Smith, and in the end, 300 cinemas in this country were equipped with the special projectors required. It was the first successful process for filming in 'natural' colour, but the colour was not printed onto the film. It was only revealed by the use of alternating red and green filters in the projectors and the cameras, and those were expensive. Inevitably, better processes were invented, where the colour was printed onto the film itself.

The first Technicolor film was produced in Hollywood in 1935. Success at the box office for Technicolor and other processes meant that from the 1960s, colour became the norm, though black-and-white films continued to be made, especially for 'art house' films.

Sound

The 'silent screen' was probably never actually silent. In the fairground 'bioscopes', the 'barker' gave a commentary, and even in the humblest picture houses there was presumably at least a piano accompaniment to the films. The bigger houses in the town centre had orchestras (see p. 24).

In their memoirs, several people recalled the 'full mechanical effects' that accompanied films at the short-lived West's Picture Palace, 1909–*c*.1916: when windows were seen being broken on screen, there was the sound of real glass being broken in the auditorium (see p. 46).

Recorded sound in cinemas took off with the advent of electrical amplification and loudspeakers. Initially this involved records played on turntables which were linked to the projectors, and the equipment was being installed from 1927 onwards. Edison's 'Kinetophone' was one such invention, but there seems to be no record of any of the Reading cinemas using it or similar systems.

The optical soundtrack came along about two years later, and this was the system that came into general use. The first talking picture to be shown in Reading was *Weary River*, at the Central Cinema, Friar Street, on 26 August 1929. According to newspaper reports, it was not entirely successful: you could hear what the hero was saying, but not the heroine.

The Pavilion Cinema in Oxford Road was designed for sound, and it opened a month later with *Show Boat*. This included songs but was not based on the musical show by Jerome Kern and Oscar Hammerstein, which gave rise to films in 1936 and 1951.

The United States got a foothold in British cinemas during the First World War, when the country was otherwise preoccupied, and the increasing predominance of American films when sound arrived was seen as a threat to film-making in this country. The coming of sound also brought specially composed film music and musical shows to the cinema.

There were many early experiments with stereophonic sound, but the first, partly successful introduction in the country came in 1953–54, when 20th Century Fox offered it along with the wide-screen CinemaScope process. Initially, Fox had stipulated that all its CinemaScope installations had to be accompanied by stereo sound, but this was abandoned fairly soon, since few cinemas could afford the whole package. Stereo gradually faded out due to the limited number of cinemas that could play it and the cost of producing the film with additional soundtracks. There is no evidence of its arrival in Reading until 1969, with the modernisation of the ABC Granby. This was using a process called Todd-AO, which used 70 mm film with a magnetic soundtrack. Though there is good evidence for this happening, it was not reported in the local papers. They reported on the opening of the licensed bar, but not the improved quality of sound and pictures!

Dolby Laboratories rejuvenated stereo in the early 1980s when they developed a system using modified optical soundtracks rather than magnetic ones, and this became the norm. 'Surround sound' was to follow, using speakers all around the auditorium.

3-D

There were occasional showings in the 1950s of 3-D films, where the audience wore special glasses. *The House of Wax*, a horror film starring Vincent Price, was the first 3-D colour picture to be released by a major American studio. In Reading, its screening at the Rex is particularly well remembered. In recent years, a new generation of 3-D films is being shown in the multiplexes.

Wide screens

Photographs of the screens in cinemas before the 1950s are often surprising. Though the auditorium might be large, sleek and streamlined, the screen is still more or less square and surprisingly small. Wide-screen processes were developed in the early 1950s to combat the increasing threat of television, which still had a small screen that was almost square. Screens wider than they were tall, corresponding to people's normal field of vision, soon became universal, though not all cinema buildings were wide enough to take them. In Reading, the Gaumont (formerly the Vaudeville) was abandoned in 1957 when it was discovered that the building was not strong enough to take the weight of a new screen.

Cinerama and CinemaScope were processes where the image was squeezed onto 35 mm film and used a special projection lens to expand it again; Todd-AO used 70 mm film for filming and projection. The first Reading cinema to install a CinemaScope screen and projectors seems to have been the Granby in January 1955, and other cinemas presumably followed shortly afterwards, though its arrival was not trumpeted in the local press. Today, Cinerama, CinemaScope and Todd-AO are almost forgotten, and the wide screen is the accepted norm.

I-Max® cinemas

Reading has never possessed one of these. They have large wrap-round screens and surround sound, and the films are made especially for them, showing off their potential and usually involving a lot of rapid movement. There are 34 such cinemas in the country, and probably more on the way.

Digital projection

The author remembers visiting the projection box of the ABC Central in the 1980s, on one of the Heritage Open Days. The film was not on reels, but lying in great coils on two large turntables, one on either side of the projector. This method of projection was eventually to change, and now most multiplexes have disposed of their 35 mm film projectors – and projectionists.

Like the move from film to digital cameras for still photography, the change from projecting from film to projection from digital data has not been welcomed by everyone, although certain advantages of digital projection are undeniable. Film distributors no longer need to maintain a fleet of vans carrying large and heavy reels of film between cinemas, and it is now possible to show films much more easily in village halls and out of doors than ever before. Nevertheless, some film devotees doubtless will still prefer the picture quality offered by film, in much the same way that some prefer to listen to music from vinyl records rather than from a CD or via the internet.

A further development has been the possibility of broadcasting live shows from theatres and opera houses direct to cinemas using satellite technology.

Part 2:
Cinemas and performances

Travelling and temporary shows, 1897–1909

Moving pictures arrived in London in 1896, produced by the Lumière brothers in Lyon, France. They were immediately popular, and the brothers soon had imitators in this country, perhaps the best-known being a firm in Blackburn, Lancashire, thanks to the BBC television programme *The Lost World of Mitchell and Kenyon*, broadcast in 2005. The surviving reels of film, showing local events, the view from a moving tramcar, people on the promenade at the seaside, or crowds of people at a football match or leaving work, were restored with astonishingly good results. Would that the 1904 film of people leaving Huntley and Palmers biscuit factory in King's Road, shown at the Town Hall, had survived!

The screenings in the Town Hall are usually reckoned to be the earliest in Reading, but there was a newspaper advertisement from an entertainer offering cinematograph shows as early as 1897 – see the section on 'Travelling Shows' in the next part of the book.

A.H. Bull's department store in Broad Street was showing films as a special attraction for the run-up to Christmas 1904.

On fairgrounds, moving pictures were shown in booths, usually with 'scientific' names like the Geo Graph, the Era Graph, the Theatregraph and the Bioscope. In front of the booth, in order to attract audiences, there might be dancing-girls, a mechanical organ or a 'barker' urging people to 'roll up!'. The experience usually cost a penny, for which audiences saw a number of short films. Travel films, reconstructions of battles in the Boer War and the funeral of King Edward VII in

1910 were popular, with the 'barker' providing a commentary. There would doubtless have been a steam-engine somewhere in the background to generate the electricity. The photograph of Arnold's Electric Bioscope and Theatre of Varieties that appears later in this book must date from this era.

Cinema in theatres, 1907–

When it opened in 1907, the Palace Theatre in Cheapside was equipped to show films. It was built as a variety theatre, and the 'bioscope' was set in operation usually at the end of the show, after the singers, comedians, magicians, jugglers, etc. Unlike its rival, the Royal County Theatre in Friar Street, the Palace Theatre never became, in effect, a cinema.

The Royal County, which opened in 1895, did not apply for a cinematograph licence until 1910. During the 1920s and part of the 1930s, cinema predominated, presumably for economic reasons. Things were changing by 1936, when the Royal County presented a mixture of stage shows and films, but early in the following year, all this came to an end when the theatre was burned down.

The Cinematograph Act, 1909

Cellulose nitrate film was flammable, and projectors were hot. In response to a number of tragedies in which buildings had caught fire and audiences had panicked in the darkness, an Act of Parliament came into force requiring all premises where moving pictures were to be shown to the public to be inspected and licensed by local authorities. Projectors had to be in fire-proof spaces, there had to be emergency lighting, and there had to be enough exits. This meant the end of travelling and temporary picture shows.

In Reading, it was usually the Chief Constable and the Chief Fire Officer who carried out the inspection and then reported back to the Watch Committee. Licences had sometimes to be withheld until necessary alterations had been carried out, and they had to be renewed annually.

The risk of fire in theatres and cinemas was – and is – taken very seriously. The author remembers visiting the ABC Central on one of the Heritage Open Days in the 1980s. There in the projection room was a notice giving the message to be relayed to the front-of-house staff if there was to be a fire. It was something like 'Is there a Mr Smith in the house?' Naturally, it would have been very unwise to shout 'Fire'!

Adapted cinemas, 1909–

In Reading, all of the early cinemas were in pre-existing buildings. In 1909 there was the Reading Picture Palace in Cross Street Hall, the King's Hall in Scowen's motor works in King's Road, West's Picture Palace in the New Foresters' Hall in West Street and the Electric Vaudeville in a gentlemen's outfitters in Broad Street. These were followed in 1911 by the Empire, Elm Park Road, in a dance-hall; the Howard Electric Theatre in a hall in Hosier Street; the Paragon in a factory that had been occupied by a manufacturing chemist in King's Road; and the Grand in Broad Street in a butcher's shop.

Purpose-built cinemas, 1911–

The first of these was the Caversham Electric Theatre, which opened in 1911, followed by the Central Cinema (1921), the Pavilion (1929), the Granby (1935), the Savoy (1936), the Rex and the Odeon (1937), and the Regal (1938). The Regal in Caversham was the last of the single-screen cinemas to be built.

The building of large suburban cinemas with more than 1000 seats in the late 1920s and 30s is a notable feature of cinema development in Reading.

Numbers of cinemas and seats, 1909–2009

From the 1920s to the 1950s, cinema-going across the country was a major pastime. Many people went to the pictures on the same night every week, and some people patronised the same cinema each time, no matter what was showing.

To give some idea of the hold that cinema-going had in Reading, the following table shows the number of cinemas in the borough, the number of screens and the approximate number of cinema seats between 1909, when cinemas were first licensed, and 2009. 1999 was the final year of the traditional single-screen cinemas.

Year	No. of cinemas	No. of screens	No. of seats
1909	3	3	1600
1919	4	4	2650
1929	5	5	5094
1939	9	9	10719
1949	9	9	10619
1959	6	6	7205
1969	5	5	6161
1979	4	7	4977
1989	2	6	2720
1999	2	6	2720
2009	1	10	2000

The numbers show that the golden age for cinema-going was about the time of the Second World War. In 1939, there were 11 buildings licensed for the showing of films. Besides the Town Halls and the Corn Exchange, there were nine cinemas: the Caversham Electric, the Central, the Granby, the

Odeon, the Pavilion, the Regal, the Rex, the Savoy and the Vaudeville. Between them, these cinemas had 10,719 seats. If there were two shows a night, that made 21,438 seats available per day. In the borough, cinemas were not allowed to open on Sundays, meaning that there were 128,628 seats available per week. The population of the borough at the time was around 133,000.

Today, although there are only 2000 cinema seats in Reading, there are more films to choose from than ever before because of the number of screens, and screenings, available every day.

Prices of admission

The 'bioscope' booths at the fair had cost a penny. The King's Hall in King's Road had cost a penny if you sat on the floor at the front, but twopence (2d.) if you wanted a chair. Cinemas in the town centre were dearer, with prices beginning at threepence (3d.). In 1914, prices at the Vaudeville, the Grand and West's Picture Palace were the same – 3d., 6d., 9d. and a shilling (1/-). Then, in 1916, to help pay for the war, Entertainment Tax was introduced, and prices increased to 9d., 1/3, 1/10 and 2/4. The Caversham Electric was always much cheaper – even with the tax, it was 5d., 9d., and 1/3.

The tax was reduced after the war. In 1939, prices were about the same as they had been in 1916. The plushier town centre houses were 9d., 1/-, 2/- and 2/6, the big suburban cinemas (Granby, Regal, Rex, Savoy) 6d., 9d., 1/- and 1/6, and the Caversham Electric 4d., 9d. and 1/3. The tax was raised again during the Second World War, but abolished in 1960. This did not stop cinemas from closing.

An old penny was worth less than half a new penny and a shilling was worth 5 new pence. The highest ticket price in 1939, 2/6 or half a crown, was worth 12½ new pence. At the time, a man working in the Huntley and Palmers' factory earned less than £3.50 a week, and a woman earned less still.

Multiplexes, 1999–

The first multiplex cinema in the country was opened at Milton Keynes in 1985, but before that, the popularity of cinemas offering a choice of films in smaller auditoria was apparent.

In Reading, the two large town-centre cinemas began conversion work in the 1970s. The ABC Central had a new auditorium built in what had been the café in 1971, and in 1977, the big auditorium was divided into two. The Odeon followed suit in 1979, with Odeon 1 (800 seats downstairs), and Odeon 2 (680 upstairs). In 1989, they found space for Odeon 3.

Also on the scene, though only briefly, were Studio 1 and Studio 2 in London Street, with 100 seats apiece, between 1972 and 1978.

Beyond the borough boundary, about six miles away by the Wokingham Road at Winnersh, the Showcase multiplex opened in November 1996 with 12 screens. This must have attracted audiences away from the more limited choices available in Reading, but by this time, after years of delay, the redevelopment of a sizeable fraction of the town centre was finally under way. The site had previously contained a large old brewery, a bus depot, warehouses, shops and a multi-storey car park. Now there emerged the Oracle Shopping Centre, complete with a ten-screen multiplex, at first called the Warner Village, which opened in 1999, when the MGM (formerly ABC Central) and the Odeon closed.

Ownership of cinemas

In the early days, cinemas tended to be owned by families, small firms and partnerships. Cinemas were making money, and entrepreneurs from other lines of business were attracted. For instance, behind the Grand in Broad Street was a partnership between William Vincent, the motor vehicle builder and agent, and Ernest Reed, the high-class gentlemen's outfitter, who had the shop next door to the cinema. When the cinema closed in 1922, Mr Vincent kept the premises on as his car showroom.

Several of the early cinemas lasted only a short time and were probably a financial loss for their owners. They tended to be slightly out of the town centre. A local photographer, W.H. Dee, was behind the Howard Cinema in Hosier Street, which lasted for only a year or so, while the Paragon in King's Road lasted for four years. This was a partnership between J.A. Lowe and G. Baker. Bio-Picture Land (later the Standard Electric) and West's Picture Palace both closed around the start of the First World War.

The Caversham Electric (later the Glendale) was started in 1911 by a partnership of five, two of them with Caversham connections and the others from Reading, while the Vaudeville was started by the White family in 1909, and the Pavilion by the Fort family in 1929.

It would appear that in the 1920s, the Caversham Electric and the Empire were under the same management: Mr C.J. Stanley was licensee of both, and the films were exchanged between the cinemas halfway through the week.

A local cinema chain, Simmons Theatres, arose in the 1930s. Walter T. Simmons and Edgar J. Simmons were the sons of Thomas Simmons, a grocer and wine merchant. In 1907, Walter, a director of Simmons and Sons, coal merchants, together with a Mr Wilson and a Mr Kingerlee, built the

Palace Theatre in Cheapside. (Mr Kingerlee's firm also built the West Reading Branch Library, now Battle Library). Mr Simmons was the manager until 1922, when he retired on health grounds. He died in 1932.

Walter Simmons' wife Mollie had a theatrical career in association with Milton Bode, the manager of the Royal County Theatre in Friar Street. She had appeared on the stage with Charlie Chaplin before he became a film star. In 1924, she became manageress of the Royal County Theatre, and 'part proprietor' for a time. She was always described as 'Mrs Walter Simmons' in the local paper, and it was she who was behind the setting up of the Granby Cinema Company to build a cinema at Cemetery Junction which she would run. The Chairman of the Granby board was Walter's brother, Edgar Simmons, who was also the architect of the cinema, and the Managing Director was Mr H. Sado.

Shortly after the Granby opened in 1935, the Palace Theatre Company and the Granby Cinema Company merged, to become Simmons Theatres Ltd. They went on to build a further three large suburban cinemas in Reading – the Savoy in Basingstoke Road in 1936, the Rex in Oxford Road in 1937 and the Regal in Church Street, Caversham, in 1938, all with Eric Norman Bailey of Maidenhead as architect, rather than Edgar Simmons. Films were swapped between the Granby in the east and the Rex in the west, and between the Regal in the north, and the Savoy in the south. However, the Simmons empire was short-lived: the Granby and the Regal went to Mayfair Cinemas as early as 1941, and the Savoy and the Rex went to ABC in 1943 – the year that Mayfair was itself taken over by ABC. The Palace Theatre, in Cheapside, which had opened in 1907, closed in 1960.

The Odeon, opening in 1937, belonged to a national chain from the outset, and other national chains were already on the Reading scene. The Vaudeville was taken over by County

Cinemas in September 1929, and the Pavilion (later Gaumont) in 1930. County Cinemas were effectively taken over by Odeon Cinemas in 1937, and J. Arthur Rank took control of Odeon in 1941, following the death of Oscar Deutsch, the founder of the Odeon chain. This meant that by 1941, with one exception, all the Reading cinemas were in the hands of two rival chains: the Rank Organisation (Odeon, Pavilion and Vaudeville) and ABC (Central, Granby, Regal, Rex, and Savoy). The exception was the Caversham Electric (later the Glendale), which finally closed in 1977.

Sunday opening

The Sunday Entertainments Act of 1932 allowed cinemas to open on Sundays, but this was subject to the will of the local authority. Reading Borough Council debated the matter in January 1937, with speeches for and against. Letters were read out from various church leaders. At the end, 16 councillors voted for Sunday opening, and 32 against. The council changed its mind in April 1940, despite much opposition, during the dark days of war. Under the Act, cinemas had to pay 5 per cent of their Sunday takings to the local authority. The local authority paid a percentage to the Cinematograph Fund and could retain the rest. In Reading, the retained proportion was distributed by the Watch Committee to local charities – around £600 a year. The Cinematograph Fund, under the control of the Privy Council, was to be used for 'encouraging the use and development of the cinematograph as a means of entertainment and instruction' – and led to the founding of the British Film Institute.

Censorship

The British Board of Film Censors was set up in 1912. Whether or not a film should be shown was decided by local authorities, and the role of the board was advisory only. Initially there were two categories: 'U', suitable for universal showing; and 'A', suitable for adults, and children accompanied by adults. In 1932, an 'H' category was added – the 'H' standing for 'horrific'. Then in 1951, the 'X' category replaced the 'H' category, and meant that the film was suitable for adults over 16 years of age only. Local authorities – the counties and county boroughs – could still ban the public showing of films in their areas and could allow the showing of unclassified films. In Reading, the Theatres Licensing Committee decided; by the 1960s it was the Watch Committee, and after that the Health and Environment Committee.

In 1938, the Theatres Licensing Committee, the Chairman of the Health Committee and the Medical Officer of Health had a private viewing of an educational film, *Marriage Forbidden*. It was aimed at preventing venereal diseases and was accepted for exhibition to adults only. In 1956, they banned the showing of *Rock Around the Clock*, starring Bill Haley and The Comets. This happened in other towns, too: this was the era of 'Teddy Boys', and cinema managers were worried about damage to their premises.

Then, in 1960, members of the Watch Committee decided to ban the showing of a film called *Peeping Tom*. This was a British horror film about a serial killer who used a portable movie camera to record the dying moments of his female victims. The distributors appealed against the decision, and a special viewing was arranged. The committee changed its mind and after that seems to have been content to follow the recommendations of the BBFC. [In 1960, it was still the British Board of Film Censors which became the British Board of

Film Classification in 1984.] In 1960, they allowed Alfred Hitchcock's film *Psycho* to be shown, which was banned in some other towns.

The situation became laughable in 1988, when the Health and Environment Committee decided to ban Martin Scorsese's *The Last Temptation of Christ*, 48 hours before it was due to open. There were complaints, so a special viewing was arranged at the ABC Central in Friar Street. The committee changed its mind. Meanwhile, Berkshire County Council's Joint Film Viewing Committee had decided to ban the film. This meant that you couldn't see it in Maidenhead, Newbury, Bracknell or Wokingham, but you could in Reading!

Local authorities retain these powers, but rarely exercise them.

Programmes

Locally shot films were popular in the early days of moving pictures, and we have already noted the showing of pictures of people leaving Huntley and Palmers biscuit factory in 1904. It is also likely that film was taken in 1910, when Lloyd George came to Reading for a mass meeting in which he spoke in favour of the Liberal candidate, Rufus Isaacs (later Lord Reading). The meeting was held in the tram-sheds in Mill Lane, which had been specially adapted for the evening to create what was probably the biggest covered open area in the town. The film, if it existed, would have been shown at the Electric Automatic Vaudeville, in Broad Street (see p. 47).

Two programmes have survived from the Vaudeville at the Berkshire Record Office, the earliest of them an illustrated synopsis of the French film called *Queen Bess*, in English, starring Sarah Bernhardt, from 1912. The film was on for a whole week and must have been considered something special to warrant a glossy booklet costing 1d. It lasted for 53 minutes, much longer than the usual fare. The other programme

CINEMAS AND PERFORMANCES

The programme of the Vaudeville for one week in June 1920.

lists the forthcoming attractions in November 1922. A third Vaudeville programme, from 1920, now in private hands, is pictured above.

At this time no 'feature film' took up most of the show: picture shows were – like variety shows in the theatre – a mixture of short items. There were normally five or six films in a show, and they changed on Mondays and Thursdays. They included a newsreel called 'Topical Budget – The News of the World in Pictures', and a 'Brief Interlude of Colour and Harmony'. This latter involved coloured lights and music from the orchestra.

The Vaudeville programme from 1920, reproduced above, shows that the 'Topical Budget' was then 'Pathé's Animated Gazette – N.E.W.S. of the World in Pictures'. The Pathé Brothers had opened their London office in Wardour Street in 1910, and their emblem at the start of each film, a crowing cockerel (which was also the emblem of France), continued to be used for many years. West's Picture Palace also showed a newsreel, the 'Animated Gazette', which boasted of sporting events – horse races, football matches, etc.

During the First World War, 'morale boosters' were shown but, as time went by and the horrors of trench warfare were becoming more generally known about, they stopped.

Feature films were becoming the norm in the 1920s. Westerns came on the scene about the same time, and with the coming of sound, films of musical shows became popular. French films stopped being shown and more American films arrived, and there were worries over the survival of the film industry in Britain. From the Cinematograph Film Act of 1927 onwards there have been Acts of Parliament requiring cinemas to show a quota of British films which have had their effect on the films shown: some of the 'quota quickies' that resulted are said to have been pretty dire.

In the early days of cinema, performances were continuous: cinemas were open between certain times, and you could arrive and go as you liked. With the coming of feature films, the programme started at set times, and there were usually first and second 'houses', with the programme being shown twice in an evening.

Children's programmes

Children's Saturday matinees have been running from the earliest days. The King's Hall in King's Road, otherwise known as the 'Penny Plunge', was running them in 1909, admission one penny.

During the Second World War, there were a lot of refugee children in town. Pressure on space in schools meant that some children had school in the mornings, and a second lot of children had school in the afternoons. It is remembered that the Granby, Regal and Rex cinemas put on free children's matinees for the children who weren't required to be in class.

The Saturday morning matinees at the Odeon and the ABC Central are fondly remembered by many from the 1950s. By this time, it cost 6d. to get in. Both cinemas ran 'clubs', and the clubs had songs; the one for the ABC was sung to the tune of the march 'Blaze Away'. The words were:

> We are the boys and girls well known as
> Minors of the ABC
> And every Saturday all line up
> To see the films we like and shout aloud with glee
> We love to laugh and have a sing-song
> Such a happy crowd are we
> We're all pals together
> We're the Minors of the ABC.

Children with a birthday were invited to go up onto the stage. The programme always included a serial and a western, and the show always ended with a 'cliff-hanger'.

In the late 1930s, the children at the Odeon were members of the Mickey Mouse Club, and there was an agreement with Walt Disney that at least one Disney cartoon would feature in each show. Their song had a particularly patriotic, war-time theme:

> Every Saturday morning, where do we go?
> Getting into mischief? Oh dear, no!
> To the Mickey Mouse Club with our badges on,
> Every Saturday morning at the O-DE-ON!
> Play the game, be honest and every day
> Do our best at home, at school, at play;
> Love King and Country will always be our song,
> Loyalty is taught is at the O-DE-ON!

Later, the Mickey Mouse Club became the Odeon Children's Club, and the song changed to:

> From far and near we're gathered here
> For the picture show.
> What delight all merry and bright
> But what we want to know –
> Is everybody happy? Yes!
> Do we ever worry? No!
> To the Odeon we have come
> Now we're all together
> We can have some fun.
> Do we ask for favours? No!
> Do we love our neighbours? Yes!
> We're a hundred thousand strong
> So how can we all be wrong?
> As members of the O.C.C. we stress
> Is everybody happy? Yes!

In the 1950s, the Reading Odeon employed 'monitors' who wore badges and got in for nothing, while others paid 6d. It was their job to see that the other children didn't put their feet on the seats.

Pianos, organs and orchestras

The small early cinemas would have had a piano accompaniment to the films. A Mrs Downing is remembered as the resident pianist at the Empire, Elm Park Road, which opened in 1911. The town centre cinemas, West's Picture Palace and the Vaudeville Electric Theatre, both had orchestras when they opened in 1909. West's advertised 'a magnificent orchestra with full mechanical effects'. The cinema did not survive the First World War.

Change of Programme every Monday and Thursday

NOTE.—Patrons are respectfully informed that Pictures of an objectionable nature will never be shown at THE VAUDEVILLE. The Management exercise the strictest censorship in the selection of pictures exhibited, which are the very latest and best procurable, all Films being seen by our representatives in London, Paris, New York, &c., &c., before coming to Reading.

THE
Vaudeville Orchestra
will play daily from
2 to 5 p.m. and 6.0 to 10.30 p.m.

#	Type	Title	Composer
1.	Overture	"The Jolly Robbers"	Suppe
2.	Selection	"Ruy Blas"	Marchetti
3.	Fantasia	"La Bohème"	Puccini
4.	Suite	"La Fete Chez Therese"	Hahn
5.	Overture	"Les Lauriers Rouges"	Marie
6.	Selection	"Cadix"	Valverde
7.	Fantasia on Melodies		Grieg
8.	Suite	"Three Light Pieces"	Fletcher
9.	Romance	"Hymne a Saint Cecile"	Gounod
10.	Overture	"Son and Stranger"	Mendelssohn
11.	Selection	"The Gondoliers"	Sullivan
12.	Fantasia	"From Italy"	Langey
13.	Suite	"Three Old English Dances"	Fiocca
14.	Hungarian Rhapsody No.1		Liszt
15.	Overture	"Semiramide"	Rossini
16.	Selection	"Popular Songs"	Lohr
17.	Fantasia	"Verbena de La Paloma"	Breton
18.	Suite	"Hibernian"	Roeckel
19.	Overture	"Don Juan"	Mozart
20.	Waltz	"Sunshine of the World"	Cuvillier
21.	Selection	"La Favorita"	Donizetto
22.	Fantasia	"Antas"	Rimsky Korsakoff
23.	Suite	"Four Indian Love Lyrics"	Woodford-Finden
24.	Saxaphone Solo	(Mr. R. Sinclair.)	

On request to the MUSICAL DIRECTOR other Selections will be played if suitable for the picture showing.
GRAND PIANO supplied by Messrs. Barnes & Avis.

Musical Director
MR. LIONEL FALKMAN,
SOLO VIOLINIST, from
THE ROYAL COVENT GARDEN OPERA CO.,
and THE NEW SYMPHONY ORCHESTRA.
LATE PRINCIPAL VIOLINIST TO
MADAME ANNA PAVLOVA.

Proprietors - W. H. White, W. J. J. Brinn.
General Manager - W. H. WHITE.

The Management reserve to themselves the right to refuse admission.

Programme from the Vaudeville, June and July 1920.

The 'Vaudy' was much longer-lived, and advertised Madame Walter's Orchestra. The programmes included an 'interval of colour and harmony', where lights came up on the orchestra as they played. Later, the orchestra was led by Lionel Falkman, formerly violinist at the Royal Opera, Covent Garden. The 1920 programme mentions a saxophone solo and a grand piano supplied by Messrs Barnes and Avis of Friar Street. The orchestra played when the films were being shown, from 2 until 5pm, and from 6 until 10.30pm daily. The pianist, Eduard Parlovitz, short in stature and affectionately known as 'Little Parlo', later took over as leader. The orchestra seems to have been very popular. Near the end of its life, in 1928, there were fifteen players. The Grand, when it opened in 1911, boasted 'a male and female orchestra', as though this was something unusual. The Central Cinema, later the ABC Central, when it opened in 1921, naturally had to have a 'first-class' orchestra: it had eight players. When sound equipment was introduced, the orchestras were disbanded.

It has been claimed that the only organ in a cinema in Reading was at the Pavilion (later the Gaumont). This appears not to have been the case: the 1921 illustrations of the interiors of the newly-opened Central Cinema and the refurbished Vaudeville (also later the Gaumont) show both of them to have had pipe organs. The newspaper descriptions of the orchestras of both cinemas include organists. The organs may have gone out of use with the coming of 'talking pictures' around ten years later. The Compton Theatre Organ at the Pavilion started up as the first talkies were arriving and entertained audiences before the show and during intermissions.

Queues, tickets, usherettes, refreshments and smoking

Going to a cinema show in one of the old single-screen cinemas involved much more human contact than it does today. First of all, you might have had to queue out into the street for popular films, with a uniformed commissionaire to keep the queue in order, and to tell you when the auditorium was full and you may as well go home. Booking and paying for tickets online was not technically possible. Instead, you bought your ticket from a lady (it always seemed to be a lady) sitting behind a glass window in the pay-box. In some cinemas, the ticket machine must have been worked by a treadle and the ticket shot up from a slot in the counter. Once inside the auditorium, you were usually shown to your seat by a uniformed usherette who held a torch to show you the way.

In the earliest days of cinema, the King's Hall in King's Road could offer you a cup of tea for a penny extra. It's not recorded whether it was served at your seat or you had to go and collect it. In later years, four of the Reading cinemas had cafés. The Central (later ABC Central) also had a dance floor, and tea dances were held; and there was a kitchen upstairs where the bread and cakes were baked. It was opened in 1921, the same year the Vaudeville was extended to include a tea-lounge. The Pavilion (later Gaumont) of 1929, and the Granby, opened in 1935, also had cafés. When the Granby was modernised in 1969, the café became a licensed bar. This was the only licensed bar in a cinema in the town.

Sweets and tobacco were on sale at most cinemas, if not all of them. When this started is not clear, and similarly, it has not proved possible to say whether ice cream was on sale from the beginning, or whether it came later. Ice cream was being produced from the 1880s and for many people has become part of the cinema-going experience.

A commissionaire at the Central Cinema, from a postcard.

By the 1950s, there was usually an intermission between the preliminaries (advertisements, news reel and a short general interest film) and the main feature film. Usherettes appeared with trays of ice cream and cold drinks in wax cartons, and queues of people seeking refreshment built up in the aisles. There was a conspiracy theory that cinemas turned up the heating before the ice-cream ladies made their appearance. The appearance of popcorn came later, in the 1970s.

An interesting sign of the times is that in cinemas of old, the seats had ashtrays screwed to the back. In modern cinemas, they have holes to take cups in the armrests. The smoking of cigarettes was commonplace in cinemas until the 1980s, although the dangers of smoking, and of breathing in other people's smoke, had been known about for more than ten years before measures began to be taken to curb the habit. From 1971, some cinemas had a compromise policy that allowed smoking on one side of the auditorium but not on the other. A film of a burning cigarette was shown to make it clear where you should be sitting if you wanted to smoke. Cinema chains banned smoking completely in the 1980s and 90s. The first one to do so in Reading was the Cannon/ABC chain in 1987. Smoking indoors in all public places was outlawed in 2007.

Closure and rebirth

The 1951 Festival of Britain must have created something of a boost for Reading's cinemas. They opened specially on the morning of 4 May, the day after the opening day, to show film of the proceedings of the day before – presumably involving processing laboratories and delivery vans working overtime.

By the time of the 1953 coronation, many more people were able to see the procession and the ceremony on the television, though only in black and white. From then on, the decline in numbers of cinema-goers became ever more apparent.

As if cinema managers had not enough to be worried about, in the second half of the 1950s, 'Teddy Boys' made their appearance. They showed off by seat-slashing, and one manager thought that the 'Teddy Girls' were as bad as the boys. Another manager is remembered for carrying out a citizen's arrest of an unruly youth and detaining him by sitting on him until the police arrived. The manager weighed 16 stone.

Various means were employed in the attempt to boost audiences. The ABC Central and the Granby tried midnight matinees, with buses laid on to take people home afterwards. The Rex tried 3-D films. The Glendale tried more adult, X-rated films, but closures seemed inexorable.

No account of Reading cinemas would be complete without a mention of 'Mr Cinema' himself: Roy Smith, a former projectionist. He had seen the building of some of the cinemas, and when they were threatened with closure he mounted campaigns and got up petitions. Over 5000 signatures were collected to save the Rex in Oxford Road, and there were also campaigns to save the Odeon and the MGM (former ABC) in 1999.

English Heritage offered a glimmer of hope. In 1999 they announced a scheme to give 'listed' status to 30 cinemas across the country. Mr Smith was hoping to get the Rex, the Odeon and the old ABC listed, but unfortunately none of those was chosen.

Then there was the suggestion that the Reading Film Theatre, held in the Palmer Lecture Theatre of the University on the Whiteknights campus, should move to the Glendale in Caversham when this closed in 1977; later, the old ABC was suggested. One report in the local paper said that the Friar Street cinema 'could be reborn as a cinema to show classics, Asian Bollywood, foreign language, art house, alternative, black and white and British movies, as well as flicks made by

Reading amateur directors and students'. The harsh reality was that the old ABC was a vast building that would need millions spent on it to put it in good order, and it sat on a site in the town centre that was itself worth many millions. The opening not many yards distant of a ten-screen multiplex in the Oracle shopping centre with adjacent car parking made closure inevitable.

In 1978, when the Studio cinemas in London Street closed, it was claimed that the big cinema chains and film distributors were squeezing the smaller operators out of the market. This may well have been so; the same thing had been said the year before by Fred Williams of the Glendale. He had difficulty in obtaining films to put on, which was one of the reasons he was closing the cinema.

Nevertheless, the wholesale closures brought about to a large extent by the convenience of having television at home did not mark the end of cinema-going. But there was a change in the kind of cinemas people expected, and maybe a change in the social demographic of the people who went to the pictures. And whatever we may think about the selection of films and 'live' shows broadcast via satellite at the Vue Cinema, there can be no doubt that more films are available in Reading than ever before.

Part 3:
The places where films were shown

Travelling shows, 1897–1909

The earliest mention of cinematic performances in the Reading area to have come to light so far is in an advertisement in the *Reading Mercury* in December 1897. This was the year after the first demonstration of moving pictures in London. 'Henri' Morley announced that he was available for 'Christmas parties and entertainments with cinematograph, Punch and Judy, conjuror, ventriloquist, etc.'. Henri Morley was none other than H.T., or Tom, Morley, in his day one of Reading's most distinguished men, who was born in 1861 and died in 1961. He was best known as an artist, designer and printer, for many years at No. 81 King's Road, but he was also a magistrate, and an antiquary and historian.

There seem to be no written records of moving picture shows in tents at the fairs that regularly visited Reading and most other towns in the early twentieth century, but we do have a photograph, reproduced here from a postcard. The picture was taken by the Reading photographer P.O. Collier, so we can be fairly certain that Arnold's Bioscope was at Reading. The word 'varieties' suggests that this was a cinema show with music hall acts as well. In the picture, we can see the 'barker' and his assistant to the left below a mechanical organ, dancing-girls in the middle, and some fellows lounging on the right – presumably the men who assembled the show and worked the equipment.

The 'bio' element of 'bioscope' is from the Greek word meaning 'life' and, consequently, movement. The King's Hall cinema in King's Road was for a short time known as Bio-Picture Land. 'Scope' has to do with 'seeing', and 'bioscope'

From a postcard by P.O. Collier.

was another name for the cinematograph, the machine that projected moving pictures onto a screen.

Reading Town Halls, Blagrave Street, 1904 –

Reading had two Town Halls, one next to the other. The first was built in the 1780s and a second, larger one was added a hundred years later. They were known as the Small Town Hall and the Large Town Hall; after refurbishment in the 1980s, they were re-named the Victoria Hall and the Concert Hall.

It is not clear which of the halls was used for the showing of pictures in 1904. The programme for 19 September that year included films of the British expedition to North Borneo, and, nearer to home, people leaving Huntley and Palmers biscuit factory in King's Road. The Borough Band played for the occasion.

When licences became necessary in 1909, both town halls had fireproof projection boxes built, and both were licensed for the showing of films. By this time, a regular visitor to the town halls was Waller Jeffs and his New Century Pictures. At 3d. and 6d., admission prices were rather high for the time. The *Chronicle* reported that 'cinematograph entertainments are a source of never-failing interest in Reading', and that one day's takings from the 'bioscope' were to be given to the mayor's soup kitchen, to help the town's many poor.

Another travelling show that came to the town halls in 1910 was Poole's Myriorama, showing animated pictures of sights of the world.

When the Small Town Hall was refurbished and re-opened as the Victoria Hall in 1989, it had an external projection box, and the electroliers were modified so that they could be raised out of the way of the projection beam. There have not been many public screenings in the hall.

A. H. Bull's department store, 52–58 Broad Street, 1904

At Christmas 1904, the Pathé Cinematograph Company of London and Paris was putting on six shows a day at A. H. Bull's, and the price of admission was one penny. The *Chronicle* said of the pictures: 'They are some of the steadiest we have seen, whilst the subjects are quite new to Reading folk'. Bull's department store closed around 1952, and the building became Wolfe and Hollander's furniture shop by 1954, which in turn became Waring and Gillow's furniture shop shortly before it was damaged by fire in 1979. A new building arose which at the time of writing houses a Next clothing shop, a shoe shop called Schuh, a River Island clothing shop, and a JD Sports.

The Palace Theatre, Cheapside, 1907–

This was a variety theatre, built as a rival to the Royal County Theatre in Friar Street, and opened on 30 September 1907. The architect was W.G.R. Sprague, who had designed several London theatres.

From the beginning, it was equipped to show films. During the early years, the 'Palace Bioscope' was in use twice nightly: there were two 'houses', at 7 and 9pm, and short films were shown as part of the variety programme, usually at the end of the bill. The Friar Street rival took to showing films a couple of years later and for a time became a cinema.

In 1937, the Palace was joined in Cheapside by the Odeon Cinema; their contrasting architectural style made them odd neighbours.

The last show at the Palace was the pantomime of 1959–60, ending on 9 January 1960. The theatre was demolished the following year, and an office block, Liverpool Victoria House, was built on the site. It is currently called Zenith House, with shops at street level.

The Reading Picture Palace, 16 Cross Street, 1909

This has been described as Reading's first full-time cinema, though it was in business for only a single month. Before and after that month, the building was the Cross Street Hall, which belonged to the Reading Liberal Association and was connected to their offices in Broad Street. It was reached by a passage between the shops at 14 and 18 Cross Street and was used for dances, lectures and the meetings of the Reading Christadelphians. A Mr L.H. Bailey, of 29 Friar Street, applied to the Watch Committee for a licence.

Nearby, and also in Cross Street, was the shop of W. Henry Dee, 'photographer and cinematographist'. He may, or may not, have been connected with the Picture Palace enterprise. He advertised that 'dissolving views, animated pictures, &c.', were available at a few hours' notice. He was certainly the man behind the Howard Electric Theatre in 1911.

At the Picture Palace there were two shows a night, at 6.30 and 8.30pm, each lasting for 90 minutes, with children's matinees on Saturdays at 3pm. Prices for adults were 2d., 4d. and 6d., and the programmes were described as 'instructive, humorous and dramatic', accompanied by 'good, appropriate music' – presumably on the piano.

The use of the Cross Street Hall for showing films may have been brought back, for a spell, in 1910, as the Electric Automatic Vaudeville. It remained a meeting hall until about the time of the Second World War, when it became incorporated into a neighbouring shop.

Its short life as a cinema was probably due in part to the fact that three rivals also opened up in 1909 – the King's Hall, the Vaudeville, and West's Picture Palace.

The King's Hall (later Bio-Picture Land and the Standard Electric Theatre), 84 King's Road, 1909–c. 1915

The building, on a site backing onto the Kennet and Avon Canal, had previously been Scowen's engineering works, which had serviced and repaired boat and road vehicle engines. In May 1909, Mr F.W. Ogden Smith applied to the Theatres Licensing Committee to build a 'cinematograph hut' – the fire-proof projection box – in the yard. At about the same time, he applied to the Drainage and New Buildings Committee for a firm of builders, Bartlett and Ross, to build an 'entrance and lantern'.

The new cinema opened in July 1909 as the King's Hall, but the name was changed to Bio-Picture Land soon afterwards, and by July of 1910 it had become the Standard Electric Theatre. The owners were now Standard Electric Theatres of London, but the manager was still Mr Smith. With only five cinemas, Standard was one of the smaller chains.

The name 'King's Hall' suggests a large room fit for a king – as well as a hall in King's Road. 'Bio-Picture Land' suggests an escape to a place of moving pictures – the Greek word 'bio' meaning 'life', and animation. 'Standard' was presumably meant to suggest high standards, rather than ordinariness.

The first shows were advertised as 'A high class and pleasing evening's entertainment for only a penny. Always the best moving pictures. Entire change of programme Wednesdays and Saturdays'. From the smaller print lower down the advertisement, it becomes obvious that if you actually wanted a seat, it would cost you twopence: a penny only entitled you to sit on the coconut matting at the front. For threepence, you could have a cup of tea during the interval. The cinema was nicknamed 'the Fleapit', and the children who frequented the coconut matting knew it as 'the Penny Plunge'.

Performances were continuous, with doors open from 6 to 10pm, Mondays to Fridays, and from 2 to 11pm on Saturdays. In December 1911, Mr Smith sought permission to open the cinema on Sunday evenings for 'cinematograph exhibitions illustrative of travels and religious subjects', but this was not granted.

Mr W.E. Woodeson, in his memoirs, had fond memories of the children's matinees here. 'The films we saw, compared with today's, were horrible. The performance seemed to move across the screen in jerks, and the film was continually breaking down. Every time this happened, the lights went up, and the lads and lasses roared out with displeasure.' He remembers that the 'huge, elderly man' employed to keep the youngsters in order had his work cut out to 'subdue the mob'. Despite the jerky pictures, the frequent breakdowns and being shouted at by the attendant, he said that 'to me, it was simply heaven'.

There do not seem to be any photographs of the building taken during its few years as a cinema, but it appears on the 1913 Goad plan, with a gas-engine and an electricity generator in a room to one side of the auditorium. It must have closed during the early years of the First World War. The 1915 street directory still shows a Mr Smith as manager, but this time it was George Smith, and it must be remembered that the information for the 1915 edition was probably collected the year before. By 1915, or soon after, the building had been taken over by the Royal Flying Corps as their mess room. In this part of town, they had also taken over some of the Sutton's Seeds buildings, and St. John's Church Hall in Fatherson Road was their lecture theatre. Today, a former office building, recently converted into apartments, with the Buzz Gym on the ground floor, occupies the site of the cinema.

The Vaudeville Electric Theatre (later the Gaumont), 47 Broad Street, 1909–1957

'The Vaudy' opened in August 1909 and by 1914 could claim to be 'the most successful picture-theatre in the provinces'. It had been converted from the former gentlemen's and boys' outfitting department of A.H. Bull's department store, which had moved along the street to No. 59, nearer to Bull's main building. The proprietors, W.H. and M. White, had opened one of the earliest cinemas in London in 1906. One of them, who was the manager at Reading, is remembered for wearing a surgical boot.

THE PLACES WHERE FILMS WERE SHOWN

The Vaudeville in its early days, from a postcard by P.O. Collier.

The name of the cinema was unusual. According to the Oxford English Dictionary, a vaudeville was originally a song from the valley of the River Vire in Normandy – the *vau de Vire*. From there it came to mean a popular song, then a kind of entertainment with popular songs in it and, in the nineteenth century, a variety show. In the United States, the vaudeville was what in Britain would have been called the music hall. In the case of Reading's Electric Vaudeville, the name was particularly appropriate, because in the early days films were short and interspersed with musical interludes.

The Vaudeville Electric Theatre, however, was built as a cinema, and not for stage shows. The auditorium was extended several times, but the Broad Street frontage seems to have

39

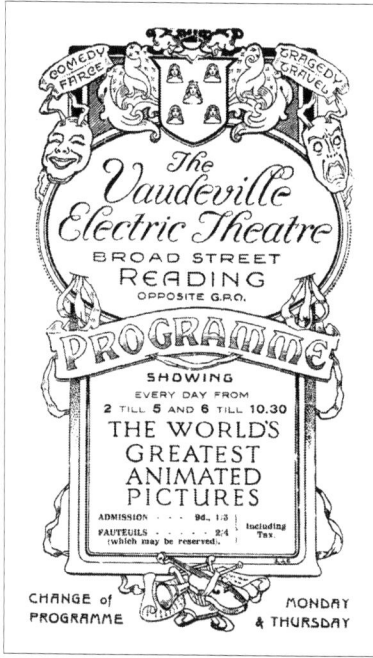

Front of a programme for June and July 1920.

remained much the same while the building was a cinema. When it opened, there were 450 tip-up seats on a sloping floor. Within weeks, the auditorium was extended over the garden at the back, and a further extension in 1913 brought the number of seats up to 1100. The Goad plan of that year shows a strip of land on the east side of the auditorium, behind the Oatsheaf public house, marked 'extension proposed, February 1913'. Then, in 1921, an even larger cinema was built, around and over the existing auditorium, but without interrupting the normal programme, bringing the number of seats up to 1457. There was a café, a tea lounge and a soda fountain. The architects for this extension were Emden, Egan and Company, of Oxford.

THE PLACES WHERE FILMS WERE SHOWN

Architect's drawing of the 1921 alterations to the front.

Advertising in 1921 said: 'The front of the theatre is of a tasteful and elegant design. The interior...marks a considerable advance on any show of the kind ever seen in Reading', and the Vaudeville was dubbed, 'Reading's Temple of Colour and Harmony'. With tip-up seats screwed to the sloping platforms, everyone had a good view of the screen, and 'two of the finest projecting machines' had been installed. There was a 'tea lounge' that was 'garbed in Old English raiment': the walls were oak panelled, and it was open from 2 until 10.15pm, Sundays excepted.

In the early days, there was a continuous performance of short films, shown between 2 and 10pm. W.E. Woodeson recalled that during the 'silent days', the Vaudeville had specialised in

The auditorium, 1921.

serial films. Soon after opening, the film *Furthest South with Lieutenant Shackleton and the British Antarctic Expedition* was especially popular: it was shown at about the time when the explorer came to give a lecture at the Town Hall. In 1914, the Pathé Brothers' latest coloured success, *In the Shadow of the Throne*, was being shown in the same programme as a locally made film, *The Stroke of the Phoebus Eight*, described as 'a thrilling drama' about the 'stroke' of a rowing crew who kidnaps his replacement. This had been shot at Henley, with the assistance of locals.

Like West's Picture Palace, the Vaudeville boasted an orchestra, which before the First World War was led by

The Vaudeville after it became the Gaumont in 1953.

Madame Walter and in the 1920s by Lionel Falkman of the Royal Opera, Covent Garden. He was succeeded as Musical Director by Eduard Parlovitz. A newspaper photograph from 1921 shows eight players, including an organist: the organ appears in the drawing of the auditorium of the same year (opposite).

The Vaudeville became part of the County Cinemas chain in 1929, which were taken over by Odeon Cinemas in 1937. J. Arthur Rank took control of Odeon in 1941. The 'Vaudy' was renamed the Gaumont in 1953 – not to be confused with the later Gaumont on the corner of Oxford Road and Russell Street.

Leon Gaumont (1864–1946) was an inventor who formed a company to manufacture movie cameras and projectors in Paris. A subsidiary company, the Gaumont-British Picture Corporation, produced films and owned cinemas across Britain, though they did not own any of the Reading cinemas. Gaumont-British became independent in 1921, and 20 years later it was acquired by Rank, so that the Rank Organisation came to 'own' the Gaumont name. It would seem that by 1953, the name of Reading's Vaudeville had become decidedly old-fashioned, and it was changed to the Gaumont. It was not to last much longer: by 1957, when the Gaumont closed, Ranks owned the Odeon and the Pavilion in Reading. The Gaumont name was transferred to the Pavilion later in the year.

As the Gaumont, the Broad Street cinema closed on 28 November 1957. There had been plans to update it, with a large new screen, but the architects had warned that the building was not strong enough to support the weight of the screen. The extent to which the building was afterwards demolished and rebuilt is unclear. It was certainly greatly modified and given a 'contemporary' front, but it appears that the roof was unchanged, and there were traces of the old cinema in the upstairs rooms. It became a branch of Timothy Whites, the chemists, and is now a branch of Boots, who took over Timothy Whites.

West's Picture Palace, 37 West Street, 1909 – c. 1916

Thomas James West must have led a colourful life. His career seems to have begun in Scotland, where, as early as 1897, he was running the Modern Marvel Company of Edinburgh, touring public halls and theatres with his cinematograph shows. In 1901 he was in Dublin, in 1902 in Bournemouth, and in 1907 he was buying leases on cinemas in Australia and

THE PLACES WHERE FILMS WERE SHOWN

No photographs of West's are known to exist, but this extract from a rather poor photograph shows an advertisement for the 'Pictures Palace' on a hoarding on the corner of Crown Street and Southampton Street.

was to become the owner of the largest cinema circuit on that continent. However, by 1909 he was back in England, where West's Picture Palace in Guildford opened in September, and his Reading Picture Palace opened on November 4.

The Palace in Reading was, appropriately, in West Street, in a building that had previously been the New Foresters' Hall. The hall had been the headquarters of the Pride of Reading Court of the Ancient Order of Foresters and was reached by a passageway between the shops. It was altered to comply with The Cinematograph Bill that was before Parliament at the time and could seat 600 in the ground floor and 150 on the balcony. West's opened on 4 November 1909 and, like the other two cinemas in the town centre – the Grand and the Vaudeville – was a 'high class' establishment with a minimum admission charge of 3d.

Competitions were held, with prizes, in order to draw in the public rather than have them patronise rival establishments. The advertising in 1909 called it 'an ideal hall, magnificently seated and comfortably warm', with music from 'a magnificent orchestra, with full mechanical effects'. It boasted, 'Travel, sport, drama, comedy, tragedy and farce – the very best films from all parts of the globe'.

One patron of the cinema was Wilfred Owen, the First World War poet, who visited it while staying with his aunt and uncle who lived at Kidmore End. In a letter sent to his mother dated 29 December 1910, he wrote: 'In the afternoon, Leslie took me into Reading to see West's Wonderful Pictures (animated)'. (Leslie Gunston, his cousin, was the architect who designed the war memorial at the main gates to the Forbury gardens.)

W.E. Woodeson remembered particularly the sound effects that accompanied the films. As a boy, he couldn't afford the threepenny, or even the twopenny cinemas, but he recalls obtaining a free ticket for West's. 'It was when a silent film showed windows being smashed. Someone at the rear of the screen duly obliged with the breaking of real glass. That was a real effect for a surprised audience'. He also remembered the novelty competitions.

The cinema closed around 1916, and Mr West died in December of that year. In October, the *Reading Mercury* had announced that 'the Foresters' Hall Picture Palace' had been acquired by a sporting syndicate and was to be known as the Reading Stadium. This was short-lived, and around 1918 the premises became the Palm Lodge – a baker's shop and cafe run by Mr G.G. Parslow. Eventually, Parslow's were to have branches all over the Reading area. The Reading Co-op eventually bought up the site and extended their central premises over it, later occupied by the Primark clothes store until 2016.

The Royal County Theatre, 113 Friar Street, 1910–1937

This theatre, at first known as the New Royal County Theatre, was converted from a place of worship, the Augustine Chapel. The architect of the conversion was Frank Matcham, the leading theatre architect of the day, and it opened on 16 September 1895. The manager, Milton Bode, applied for a cinematograph licence in March 1910, and for a time, in the 1920s and early 1930s, it was used entirely for the showing of films. By 1936 there was a mixture of stage and screen shows, but then disaster struck during the running of the pantomime in 1937: the theatre burned down in the early hours of the morning of 7 January, and it was not rebuilt. The Littlewood's department store built on the site extended through to Broad Street. The theatre site is now occupied by the Comedy Loft and the Bowery District night club.

The Electric Automatic Vaudeville, 27 Broad Street, 1910

The only evidence for the existence of the Electric Automatic Vaudeville seems to be the photograph of 1910 (overleaf), which was intended to show the Parliamentary candidate for Reading, Rufus Isaacs, on the balcony of the Liberal Club. It happens also to show the entrance to what must have been a temporary cinema: a notice below the big sign reads, 'Open for a few weeks only'. In fact, the Automatic Vaudeville could well have been in Cross Street Hall, which belonged to the Reading Liberal Association and the year before had been the

The Electric Automatic Vaudeville, 1910, with Rufus Isaacs and his wife on the balcony.

short-lived Reading Picture Palace. It could be reached from the Liberal Club offices in Broad Street as well as from Cross Street. Maybe the film-show was part of the electioneering campaign and was 'automatic' inasmuch as the same films were shown again and again. It is tempting to think that moving pictures might have been taken at the big meeting of the Reading Liberals in the tram-sheds in Mill Lane, with David Lloyd George and Mr Isaacs present, on New Year's Day of 1910; but this is mere speculation. The Liberal Club premises have since been incorporated into the HSBC Bank (formerly the Midland Bank), and the balcony is no more, though there is still a doorway below where the balcony was.

THE PLACES WHERE FILMS WERE SHOWN

The Empire Picture Theatre, Elm Park Road, c. 1909 – c. 1930

The building in a street of terraced houses in West Reading dated back to the development of the Elm Park Estate and may well have been the Temperance Refreshment House designed for Mr E.J.S. Jesse by the architect G.W. Webb in 1888, mentioned in Sidney Gold's book on Reading architects. Street directories show that it was a Salvation Army Hall between 1894 and 1902, a Wesleyan Mission Hall between 1903 and 1905, a bicycle factory run by John Reeves in 1906 and 1907, the Elm Park Hall Dancing Academy between 1909 and 1911 and the Empire Picture Theatre from around 1909, which operated for about 20 years. 'Empire' was a rather grandiose name for a small cinema in a quiet residential street.

W.E. Woodeson remembered it being very popular in its heyday. It was known to children as 'the Twopenny Plunge',

The building which had been the Empire Cinema, c. 1985.

49

where for a small price they could sit on the floor at the front. A Mrs Downing is remembered as the resident pianist.

Frederick Sherman was the first licensee, but the 1922 directory shows that the proprietors were then R. Rosbottom and L.W. Dearden. By this time it must have shared a film booking agency with the Glendale in Caversham, and Mr C.J. Stanley was licensee of both cinemas. The licence lapsed between 1930 and 1931.

After the cinema closed, the building became Alfred Matthews' mineral water factory. This lasted until around 1979, and towards the end Mr Matthews advertised himself as a bottler of Pepsi-Cola. Finally it was a tyre depot, and then, around 2005, it was demolished and houses were built on the site.

The Caversham Electric Theatre (later the Glendale), Church Street, Caversham, 1911–1977

The Caversham Electric opened in January 1911 with 500 seats and Edward Bennett as licensee. It was built on part of the former playground of the Caversham House Academy, as was the public library next door. The drawing of the cinema by local architect Ernest Ravenscroft (right) which was published in the *Reading Standard* of January 1911 cannot have been what was actually built. The partners in the enterprise were William Thomas Fidler and J.St.L. Stallwood of Caversham, and E.A. Vince, John Sawyer and S.G. Chamberlain of Reading.

The pay-box and iron staircases going up to the balcony were under an arch, but open to the street. The projection box was reached by an iron ladder at the side of the building, and people remember that in hot weather the projectionist would leave the door open, so that he could be seen at work. From a later era, others remember that during cold weather in the 1950s customers were turned away because the projectors had frozen!

THE PLACES WHERE FILMS WERE SHOWN

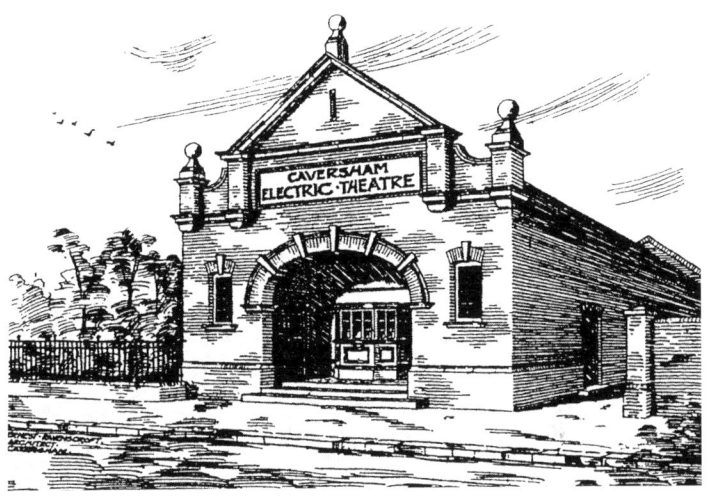

The Glendale, as first envisaged but not as built.

When the Empire in Elm Park Road was in business (until c.1930), the Caversham Electric must have been using the same film booking agency, because films that appeared in one cinema moved to the other a few days later. The licensee of both cinemas was Mr C.J. Stanley.

Mr Stanley is remembered as being very much in command, insisting on closing all the window shutters himself before each show and ensuring that everyone was seated before he would nod to the projectionist, and the show could begin. At children's matinees, they would try to hit him with their pea-shooters in the dark. Then the lights would go up and the children would be searched. Any child in possession of a pea-shooter was made to stay behind afterwards and sweep up the peas.

After 1944, there was a change in ownership. Fred Williams and his brother-in-law took over, and the cinema closed for a spell, to re-open as the Glendale. The local paper announced,

The Glendale in its early days, with Caversham Library to the left.

'Reading's intimate cinema will shortly be opening. The Electric Theatre, Caversham, closed June 4th for re-decoration and renovation. The theatre has been taken over by Glendale Theatres Corporation Ltd., London, and will in future be known as the "Glendale" Theatre, Caversham. We shall bring to our Caversham audiences the best Britain and

THE PLACES WHERE FILMS WERE SHOWN

The Glendale, at some time between 1944 and 1947.

Hollywood can offer.' There do not appear to have been any other Glendale cinemas in the country. Mr Williams was to remain there for 33 years, until the cinema closed.

It seems likely that the 'Glendale' name was chosen not just because it was a pleasant-sounding name for a picture house situated in a valley, but also because in the 1930s, Hollywood film stars were routinely photographed at the Grand Central Air Terminal at Glendale, a Los Angeles suburb.

W.E. Woodeson remembered that before the 1944 renovation, the seats faced away from the street, but afterwards they faced Church Street. Presumably this means that the projection box had been moved.

Following the change of name in 1944, the cinema was re-fronted in 1947, bringing the pay-box and stairs inside the building. The seating was reduced from 500 to 400.

In the 1960s and 70s, the Glendale showed films the second time round: a few months after they had been shown at the ABC or the Odeon, they would turn up here. It was always cheaper than its rivals, with admission prices about half those of the town centre cinemas. It certainly saw off its rival across the road, the Regal, which lasted for only 20 years, from 1938 to 1958. The Glendale battled on until 1977, towards the end showing X-rated films in the hope of boosting audience numbers. It closed on 4 June, and the building was bought by the New Testament Church of God, who still own it. (The former Gaumont Cinema in Oxford Road is also now a church.)

The Paragon Electric Theatre, 29 King's Road, 1911–1913

James Alfred Lowe of 42 Oxford Road applied for a cinematograph licence in February 1911, but was at first turned down. The Chief Fire Officer, who carried out an inspection, reported that the building – formerly the factory of Bradley and Bliss, manufacturing chemists – had been adapted by Mr Lowe and by a Mr G. Baker. They proposed generating their own electricity using a steam traction engine in the yard, rather than buying it from the Reading Electricity Supply Company. The traction engine would constitute a nuisance, and the application was refused. Less than a week later, Mr Lowe sent in a letter, signed by 18 people living nearby, saying that they did not mind the traction engine in the yard, and the licence was granted.

The name 'Paragon' suggests a place that is excellent, a model of its kind. Nevertheless, it lasted for only three years or so. It was never as popular as the Standard over the road. It was a 'twopenny house' and beyond the means of youngsters, as W.E. Woodeson recalled, and it only appears in the street directories for 1912 and 1913. The Goad plan of 1913 has the words, 'Alterations proposed for billiard saloon, Feb. 1913' written over the site. The Reading Billiard Hall burned down in 1928, after which Julian's built a car showroom on the site. No photographs of the building as a cinema are known to exist, and the site now must be underneath the office building originally called King's House, but at the time of writing has been re-named the White Building and has had all its windows replaced.

The Howard Electric Theatre, Hosier Street, 1911–c. 1913

The building started as the Hosier Street Mission Hall, which was there from 1887 to 1890, after which it became the Beaconsfield Club. From around 1910 it was the Howard Hall, presumably so-called because of its proximity to the corner of Howard Street. Then, in 1911, the local photographer William Henry Dee obtained a cinematograph licence for the building, and it became the Howard Electric Theatre, though it only lasted for a short time. Mr Dee's shop in Cross Street advertised 'dissolving views, animated pictures, etc., arranged at a few hours' notice'. He is on the electoral roll at his house in Armour Road in Tilehurst until 1913, but doesn't appear in 1914. The manager was Henry Charles Hemming, who is remembered by W.E. Woodeson.

This was a small cinema that seems never to have advertised in the local paper, and it only appears in directories for 1912 and 1913. After that the building was again the Howard Hall. From 1920 onwards it was occupied by John Mares Ltd., wholesale clothiers, and between 1936 and 1962 it was the bakery of Mares and Company. After that, the whole area was redeveloped, with the Hexagon covering the site of the cinema.

The Grand, 100–101 Broad Street, 1911–1922

The building, designed by the local architect G.W. Webb, is still there, with the date 1904 at the top of the gable. It was occupied by Collins and Son, butchers, poulterers and fishmongers, before its conversion to a cinema. Behind the conversion were two local businessmen, William James Vincent, of Vincent's the coachbuilders and motor vehicle agents in Castle Street, and Henry Ernest Reed, the high-class gentleman's outfitter who had the shop next door at No. 99. The cinematograph licence was granted subject to additional fire-proofing and the provision of an additional emergency exit in Chain Street.

The first advertisement in the local paper appeared in the *Chronicle* of 30 December 1911 – by which time it had already opened. Admission prices were 3d., 6d., 9d. and 1/-, with continuous performances between 2 and 10pm, six days a week. This cinema was the only one in Reading to have Kinemacolor projectors. The advertisement boasted that Kinemacolor was 'the only natural colour process in the world, as exhibited at the Scala Theatre in London, and by Royal command' (see p. 5).

W.E. Woodeson recalled that the seats at the Grand faced Broad Street, and that during the First World War it was not unusual to see queues of people waiting to get in at both the Broad Street and Chain Street entrances. He remembered Mr Hermon Turner as manager at this time.

The Grand closed in 1922, and the building became Vincent's car showroom until they opened their state-of-the-art showrooms in Station Square in 1928. After that, the building became the Cadena Café and later Knight's the newsagents. At present it is a branch of the Santander Bank.

The Grand in Broad Street, with a passing electric tramcar, *c.* 1920.

The entrance, complete with commissionaires and potted palms.

The London Street Pavilion, 112 London Street, from 1920

A 'pavilion' was originally a tent. From there it came to mean a light, moveable building, a building used to shelter from rain, and then a building used for entertainment.

In December 1920, Henry Egby took out a cinematograph licence for the Pavilion. Though he never seems to have advertised in the local papers, it must have run for a few years. W.E. Woodeson wrote that Mr Egby was in fact renting St Giles's Hall, which was reached by a passageway between two shops. The building had been used as a chapel by the Methodists and the Baptists before becoming St Giles's (Church of England) Hall. According to Mr Woodeson, the cinema's Saturday morning matinees were very popular with young people in the neighbourhood.

The cinema seems to have been short-lived: in 1929, a much larger Pavilion cinema was built on the corner of Oxford Road and Russell Street (see p. 63). The hall in London Street became the Foresters' Hall, and in the 1970s it became the After Dark nightclub. In 2016, the building was threatened by developers intent on constructing flats on the site. The planning application was refused but devotees of the nightclub continue to be apprehensive.

The Tilehurst Cinema, 15 Victoria Road, Tilehurst, 1920 – c. 1929

This was another small venue. Frank William White, of 'Clovelly', Westwood Road, Tilehurst, applied for a cinematograph licence for the Village Hall in December 1920. The granting of the licence was delayed until the necessary work had been completed the following month. In December 1921, the licence was transferred to a Mr Edward P. Naylor, of 'Cranford', Westwood Road, Tilehurst. In its adverts, the address is never given – it is just 'Tilehurst Cinema – Healthy Interest Pictures Perfectly Projected'. It operated on Mondays and Fridays at 7.30pm. Children under 16 could get in for 2d., and for grown-ups, tickets were 5d., 9d., 1/- and 1/6d. In such a small hall, one wonders what the difference was between a fivepenny ticket and one costing one-and-six! The licensee in 1928, Thomas Morgan, applied to use the Arthur Hill Memorial Baths near Cemetery Junction as a cinema by installing temporary wooden flooring between October and April, when the baths were closed. His application was refused in November by the Parks and Pleasure Grounds Committee, which also looked after swimming baths. The licence for Tilehurst Village Hall was later transferred to Mr John Arthur Galliers and lapsed between 1929 and 1930.

The Central Cinema (later the ABC Central, the Cannon, and the MGM), Friar Street, 1921–1999

This was built on the site of Tompkins's horse repository and opened 21 March 1921. The architect was George Gardiner of Oxford. The front of the building – the only part that could be seen from the street – was in the 'New Greek Style', clad in a kind of glazed white faience called 'Marmo', with attached pillars above and three cast-iron flambeaux above the parapet, with electric lights. The effect, when the electric torches were lit at night, must have made Friar Street look like ancient Athens. On the ground floor, one half of the building contained the foyer and the other a shop. In the early years it was occupied by Fidler's seeds and afterwards became the Crystal Room slot-machine arcade.

It was a big cinema. Accounts vary as to the number of seats, but there were around 1400. The photograph looking towards the proscenium at the time of opening shows organ-pipes on either side (see p. 61), and the description of the orchestra

PICTURE PALACE TO PENNY PLUNGE

The Central Cinema, with pillars and electric flambeaux, c. 1955.

published in the local paper mentions violins, violas, double bass, tympani and drums, and an organ. The leader was Mr H. Errington, the Lyons' Popular Café pianist. It had a café, kitchens to cook the bread and cakes, and a dance-floor with a small platform for the orchestra. Customers could enjoy a tea-dance before the show – the band, presumably, had to play during the film as well as for the dancing.

The Central was the first Reading cinema to show talking pictures. *Weary River* was shown on 26 August 1929, though the sound was not a total success.

From the post-war era, children's Saturday morning matinees are well remembered, and the 'ABC Minors' had their own song (see p. 23).

In 1971 a second auditorium with 226 seats was built in the former café, and in 1977 the big auditorium was divided

THE PLACES WHERE FILMS WERE SHOWN

The auditorium, from the back of the circle and from the stage, 1921.

The frontage in 1979.

into two, creating a 'Luxury Lounge' downstairs with 534 seats and a smaller auditorium in what had been the circle, with 180 seats. Around this time, the manager Fred Crossley had a reputation for innovative programming that brought audiences flocking; this included late-night screenings on Fridays. He retired in 1990, after 20 years at the ABC.

The take-over by Associated British Picture Corporation – the ABC chain – had come about in 1935: advertisements in the local papers show the ABC and triangle logo from

September onwards. When ABC took over the Granby in 1943, it became necessary to distinguish between the two, and the Central became the ABC Central. In the 1980s there was a complicated series of take-overs, with Warner Brothers disposing of their shares in ABC, ABC being sold to Electrical and Musical Industries (EMI), and EMI selling it on to the Cannon Cinemas Group in 1986; and so the Friar Street cinema became the Cannon. Only a few years later, Cannon Cinemas were bought by Pathé Communications, who also bought what was left of Metro-Goldwyn-Mayer (MGM); and so, in 1994, the Cannon became the MGM.

It closed on 22 March 1999, in advance of the opening of the multiplex in the Oracle shopping centre. There was a proposal to move the Reading Film Theatre into the building and show a wide range of different films there, but in the end this came to nothing. The cinema was demolished, along with The Boar's Head pub and the small shop next door, to be replaced by a monstrous concrete building housing the Ibis and Novotel hotels.

The Pavilion (later the Gaumont), Oxford Road, 1929–1979

Built by Pavilion (Reading) Ltd., this opened on 21 September 1929. The managing director of the company was Mr R. Fort, and the resident manager (who in fact lived in a house called 'Ashfort' in Farnborough) was Mr R.F. Fort. This was the first of the Reading cinemas to be built with talking pictures in mind: the architect was Harold S. Scott of Birmingham. There was a 'diffused lighting system', since the management realised that glaring light was harmful to the eyes, and there were 1380 seats. There was a tea lounge, and before the show you could enjoy Norman Tilley 'at the Pavilion's mighty organ'. When Mr Tilley wasn't available, George Pettingell,

The Pavilion, shortly after opening.

The auditorium from the stage.

Specially decorated lorry to promote Show Boat in Valpy Street.

organist at Holy Trinity Church across the road, would come over and entertain audiences with the musical hits of the day; Leslie Davies, the official Borough Organist, also deputised. The organ was removed in 1960 and taken to the basement of a shop in Ventnor on the Isle of Wight, where it was restored.

Showboat was the first picture to be screened – with sound, and the beginning of 'a new era in entertainment', as the advertising ran. A lorry decked out to look like a Mississippi paddle-steamer drove around the town to promote the film (above).

The Pavilion was acquired by County Cinemas in 1930, and County Cinemas themselves were taken over by Odeon Cinemas in 1937. J. Arthur Rank took control of Odeon in 1941, and two days after the closure of the Gaumont Cinema in Broad Street on 28 November 1957, the Oxford Road cinema was renamed the Gaumont. After it closed on 21 April 1979, the Pavilion/Gaumont became the Top Rank Bingo Hall, and following the closure of the bingo hall on 21 April 1989, the building was converted to become the Riley Snooker Centre. This in turn closed in 2011. In 2013 the building was again converted and re-opened as the LifeSpring Church, with a large 'Pavilion' sign on the front.

The Granby (later ABC Granby and ABC London Road), 1935–1982

Named after the nearby Marquis of Granby public house, this cinema was built by the Granby Cinema Company Ltd., whose chairman was Edgar Simmons, also the architect who designed the building. On the board was his sister-in-law, who always seems to have been known as Mrs Walter Simmons, and who was to manage it. A year or so after the opening, in 1935, the company had become Simmons Theatres Ltd. and went on to build a further three cinemas in Reading – the Savoy, the Rex and the Regal.

The Granby, at the time of opening.

The newspaper report of the opening on 3 September 1935 said that the Granby 'would fulfil a long-felt need in the rapidly developing East End of Reading'. There were 1177 seats, and no expense had been spared in its construction. It boasted a 'steel screen' – only the second of its kind in the country, the other being at the Regal, Marble Arch, in London. It was claimed that this screen 'contributed depth to the picture and quality to the sound'. The acoustics of the auditorium had been a special consideration, and the air was to be washed and purified using special apparatus. The cinema also had a café.

The opening night at the Granby. Seated: Mrs. Walter Simmons (manageress); Edgar Simmons (chairman and architect); John Kay (director), whose firm had built the cinema; Mr H. Sado (managing director); and Mr W.L. Agar (director).

The ornate Art Deco interior of the Granby from the back of the auditorium.

The Granby seems to have been at the forefront of cinema development in Reading. It was the first to install a wide screen, in 1955. After its modernisation in 1969, it had 70mm projection equipment and stereophonic sound, and it was the only cinema in town to have a licensed bar. But this modernisation led to the loss of much of the original Moorish but slightly jazzy decoration. As the *Reading Chronicle* of 9 May reported, 'The ornate decorations of the thirties, decorated frieze and marble columns are to go, and the foyer is to be opened up to give an impression of space'.

The Granby was sold to Mayfair cinemas in 1941, who were themselves acquired by the ABC chain in 1943, after which the name of the cinema was changed to ABC Granby

The auditorium from the stage.

in an attempt to avoid confusion with the ABC Central in Friar Street. By 1979, the name had been changed again, to ABC London Road. It closed on 27 November 1982 and was demolished.

The Marquis of Granby in question was John Manners, who lived between 1721 and 1770. He was a famous soldier in the Seven Years' War who looked after the well-being of his men and so earned their respect, and he had many pubs named after him. The long-established Granby pub near Cemetery Junction closed in 2012 and recently became an ice-cream parlour, though the name lives on in Granby Court, an apartment block built on the site of the cinema.

The Savoy, Basingstoke Road, 1936–1961

Affectionately known as 'the Cabbage', it opened on 20 March 1936, with 1044 seats. It was the second cinema in the Simmons chain to be built, and the architect was Eric Norman Bailey, who also designed the third and fourth cinemas, the Rex and the Regal. W. Tindall, the builder, completed the work in 16 weeks, and in the report of the opening in the local paper, the Simmons spokesman said that the Savoy would 'fulfil a long-felt need'. According to the local paper, Whitley was 'virtually a new town, but without local facilities'.

Besides the vegetable, the word 'Savoy' suggests opulence and comfort. Savoy is a region of south-eastern France, and in London the name was given to a grand medieval palace

The Savoy, shortly before it opened.

THE PLACES WHERE FILMS WERE SHOWN

The opening night at the Savoy. Left to right: A.R. Parker (manager); G. Kitchener (chairman), the Mayor, W.H. Bale; E.N. Bailey (architect); Alderman Mrs Alice Jenkins; W. Tindall (builder), the Mayoress, Mrs W.H. Bale; Councillor W.E.C. McIlroy; F J. Parker (managing director); and Councillor H.V. Kersley.

The curved and coved interior of the Savoy.

that was destroyed during the Peasants' Revolt of 1381. Later, King Henry VII founded a hospital in the area. The Savoy Theatre opened in the same area in 1881, and the Gilbert and Sullivan operas brought in such large profits for the impresario Richard D'Oyly Carte that he was able to build the adjacent Savoy Hotel in 1889, the last word in luxury.

Several actors must have been living nearby in the late 1950s – Robert Beatty, Alastair Sim and George Cole are remembered as regular patrons at the Savoy.

It was sold to the ABC chain on 18 January 1937, less than a year later after opening. It was closed on 12 August 1961 and demolished. By 1972 a Fine Fare supermarket was on the site, and at the time of writing it is a Cotswold outdoor activity store.

The Odeon, Cheapside, 1937–1999

The first cinema to be called the Odeon in Britain was built in Birmingham in 1930 by Oscar Deutsch, son of a scrap metal merchant. In Ancient Greece the words 'odeon' and 'odeum' referred to a building for musical performances. The Odeon Theatre in Paris opened in 1782, and the name was used for cinemas on the continent from the 1920s. By the time of Deutsch's death in 1941, there were 258 Odeon cinemas, forming one of the largest cinema chains in the country. His widow sold them to J. Arthur Rank, who at the time was forming the Rank Organisation. It was jokingly reckoned that the letters 'ODEON' stood for 'Oscar Deutsch Entertains Our Nation'.

The Reading Odeon was a classic of its kind, designed by Mr A. Percival Starkey of Harrow, who had originated the 'Odeon Style' – lots of curves and coving, with cream-coloured faience tiles on the front – in 1933. The local paper, inexplicably, described it as 'fitting in perfectly with its

The Odeon, shortly before opening. The road to the car park, below the lounge, is to the right.

surroundings'. It mentioned a spacious balcony lounge built over the road to the car park; this must have been the only Reading cinema with its own car park. The lounge had settees and chairs where patrons could wait for their friends. 'The heating and ventilation for the theatre is in accordance with the latest ideas. Fresh air is drawn in from a high position in the Thorn Street front, and proceeds in a shaft to the basement, though a heater controlled to raise the temperature to a suitable level. It is then blown into the auditorium via the decorative grilles. ... Vitiated air is drawn through the troughs of the light-fittings'. The report went on to mention

The large, coved auditorium from the back of the circle, with what appears to be a small, square screen, as they all were at the time.

the 'world-famous Thomson-Houston wide-range talking picture apparatus'. There were 1210 seats in the stalls and 494 on the balcony, a total of 1704, making the Odeon the biggest picture-house in town.

The Odeon was opened by the local MP, Dr A.B. Howitt, on 8 March 1937. Also present were the Mayor of Reading, Alderman Mrs Alice Jenkins, and Oscar Deutsch, the head of the Odeon chain. Music for the occasion was provided by the Band of the Scots Guards. Whether they played in the auditorium or out in the street is not recorded.

Next door to the Reading Odeon was the Palace Theatre, and with popular shows people sometimes found themselves in the wrong queue. Children's Saturday matinees are remembered with particular pleasure, together with their songs (see p. 23).

THE PLACES WHERE FILMS WERE SHOWN

The auditorium from the stage.

The opening night at the Odeon. Seated, left to right: Miss Olwen Roose (Mrs H. Kerr); the Mayor, Alderman Mrs Alice Jenkins; Mrs F. Stanley Bates. Standing: a page boy (possibly Gerry Prescott); Mr H. Kerr (manager); Mr A.P. Starkey (architect); Mr Christopher Stone; Dr A.B. Hewitt MP; Mr Oscar Deutsch (chairman of Odeon Theatres Ltd.); Mr W.G. Elcock; and Mr F. Stanton Bates.

A notable character at the Odeon was Gerry Prescott, known as 'the Chief'. He started as a page boy when the cinema opened and retired in 1987, by which time he had been chief projectionist for 36 years. His 50 years' service was interrupted only briefly by military service during the Second World War.

At the death of Oscar Deutsch in 1941, the Rank Organisation took control of the Odeon chain, but the old name was retained. The interior was redecorated in 1967, and in 1979 the auditorium was divided into two, with Odeon 1 downstairs (800 seats) and Odeon 2 upstairs (680 seats). In 1989 a third screen was added. The cinema closed on the evening of Sunday, 28 November 1999; the Warner Village multiplex at the Oracle had opened on the previous Friday. The Reading Odeon was the last of the old-style cinemas to go. An apartment block was built on the site in Cheapside – called, ironically, the Picture House.

The Rex, Oxford Road, 1937–1958

The third of the cinemas built by Simmons Theatres, the Rex was built in 15 weeks by Fassnidge, Son & Morris. Like other Simmons cinemas, the owners claimed that it had been built 'to fulfil a long-felt need in this part of Reading', and they pointed out its proximity to many new houses and trolley-bus and bus stops. Like the Savoy and the Regal, it was designed by the architect Eric Norman Bailey. There were 1100 seats, 800 in the stalls and 300 upstairs in the 'Stadium'. The Rex had air conditioning and claimed to be 'the last word in comfort and efficiency'. The opening night was on 29 September 1937. On the front, there were three blue neon tubes along the top, and the word 'Rex' was spelled out in neon lights. The name, like that of the Regal, which opened a year later, suggested somewhere that was fit for a king, or maybe 'a king among cinemas'.

THE PLACES WHERE FILMS WERE SHOWN

The Rex, at the time of opening.

On the newspaper photograph (above) taken around the time of opening, the words 'Louis' and 'Farr' appear on a banner over the top, advertising the British Movietone News film of the fight between Joe Louis and Tommy Farr, which had taken place in New York on 30 August 1937.

PICTURE PALACE TO PENNY PLUNGE

The auditorium of the Rex.

The Rex was sold to the ABC chain on 14 August 1943 and closed on 18 October 1958. For a time, the building was used by John Filbee's second-hand car business and was then occupied by Lockhart Catering Equipment Ltd. It was damaged by fire, and demolished in September 2000. An apartment block, Winslet Place, now stands on the site; its name preserves the connection of the site with cinema – the actress Kate Winslet was born in Reading in 1975.

The Regal, Church Street, Caversham, 1938–1958

This was the fourth and last cinema to be built by Simmons Theatres, and the last of the single-screen cinemas to be built in Reading, opening on 3 October 1938. Like the Savoy and the Rex, it was designed by the architect Eric Norman Bailey. It had 857 seats and is remembered for being 'posher' and 'plushier' than the Glendale across the road. The name itself suggested somewhere palatial, fit for a king. The higher admission prices, compared with its 500-seat rival over the road, probably account to some extent for its short existence of just under 20 years.

Photographs of the Regal are few and far between – this one is copied from a newspaper.

Regal House, shortly before demolition.

Like the Granby, it was sold to ABC in 1943. Closure came on 7 June 1958, after which the building was used as warehouse and offices. Regal House, as it became known, was demolished in October 1982, and a Waitrose supermarket was built on the site.

Reading Film Theatre, The Palmer Building, University of Reading, Whiteknights Park, 1970–

There was a precursor to the Reading Film Theatre: the Reading Film Society, which met in the Abbey Gateway and advertised its programmes in the local papers around 1953.

The Reading Film Theatre operated for many years in a much larger hall. When it opened in 1970, the RFT was sponsored by the University of Reading, Reading Borough Council and the British Film Institute. It was opened by Mai Zetterling, the Swedish actress and director, and screenings have continued in the 409-seat Palmer Lecture Theatre for over 40 years. With the closure of the last of the town-centre single screen cinemas in 1999, it was suggested that the RFT might move to the former ABC, but this was not to be. The Film Theatre's aim is to show the best films from around the world, and although it operates only during the university term time, it is open to everyone.

The Palmer Building in 2017.

Studios 1 and 2 (Studio 1 later became Studio X), London Street, 1972–1978

These two small cinemas, with 100 seats apiece, opened on 19 July 1972. They were operated by the Star Group, a company based in Leeds, and were on the first floor of the building, above part of the Olympia Bingo and Social Club. The building had been the Olympia Ballroom and is now the Shenai Olympia Ballroom, a venue for dinners, wedding receptions and corporate events. In 1975, Studio 1 became a members-only cinema club, Studio X, showing unclassified films. When both Studios closed on 18 February 1978, the Bishop of Reading was reported to have said, 'I'm glad to hear of it'.

Studios 1 and 2, around the time of opening.

The Hexagon, 1977–

Around 1970, the Borough Council was planning to leave the municipal buildings, including the town halls, in Blagrave Street and sell them off to developers. On the other side of the town centre there were to be new civic offices, a cultural centre containing the library, museum and art gallery, a theatre, and a concert hall; but the only part of the scheme to be built as planned was the Civic Offices, which were demolished during 2016. The cultural centre failed to materialise, leaving the museum and art gallery in the old buildings, while the library moved to its present location on the corner of King's Road and Abbey Square. Instead of a separate theatre and a concert hall, a multi-purpose hall – the Hexagon – was decided upon. Many have said that is not ideal, either as a concert hall or as a theatre, and the Council is currently seeking a partner to build a replacement.

The Hexagon opened in November 1977 with 1650 seats. It was built with projection facilities but has been used only occasionally to show films. The author remembers the film of Charles Dickens's *Little Dorrit*, starring Alec Guinness, Derek Jacobi and Max Wall, being shown on a Sunday afternoon and evening in 1989. It lasted 360 minutes, or 6 hours!

The Warner Village (later Vue), The Oracle, 1999

This was opened, as part of the Oracle shopping centre, on 3 November 1999 by the television presenters Dale Winton and Anthea Turner. The Warner Village was a multiplex with ten screens and 2000 seats between them; the largest auditorium had 380 seats and the smallest 86. When it opened, there was a promise that one of the screens would be dedicated to 'non-mainstream' films. It had a 24-hour licence, reckoned to be necessary because they could only fit in three 'blockbusters'

The Warner Village, about the time of opening.

screenings an evening. With its 'premiere-sized' screens and 'love seats' with retractable armrests, it would rival the recently-opened Showcase multiplex at Winnersh.

The Warner Village chain was a joint venture between Warner Brothers International Theatres, based in the US, and Village Roadshow in Australia. By the time they were acquired by SBC International Cinemas in 2003, there were 36 'Warner Villages' in this country. They were rebranded as Vue cinemas the following year. It seems a strange choice of name – people seem unsure as to whether to pronounce 'vue' in the French way, or like the English word 'view'.

The Forbury Hotel, 2004 –

The Shire Hall, built in 1911, was abandoned by the County Council when it moved out to Shinfield Park in 1980. The building was later converted to become the Forbury Hotel in 2004. It includes a private cinema for presentations, lectures and private film screenings which can seat up to 30 on Italian leather seats.

Outdoor cinema

In the past, open-air cinema would have seemed alien to this country: it was something you might come across on holiday in Mediterranean countries, but the British climate really was not suitable. This attitude seems to have been disproved by a firm called Cult Screens, which has shown films in Caversham Court Gardens during the summer months since 2013. The screen is set up on the lawn by the river, and there are bean bags, deckchairs, refreshments and a licensed bar.

St. Martin's Precinct, Church Street, Caversham – ?

Plans were revealed in 2014 for an upgrade of the shopping precinct in the middle of Caversham, which was to include a small cinema. With nearby car parking likely to be available in the evenings and a relatively prosperous catchment area, a cinema seemed a viable possibility. In September 2015, Waitrose announced that they were no longer going ahead with the extension to their existing supermarket originally envisioned as part of the plans for the precinct. Hermes Real Estate, the owners of St Martin's, said refurbishment on a smaller scale would still happen. It will be interesting to see what transpires; if a cinema is built, it will be very close to the former site of the Regal and across the road from the former Glendale.

Films made in or near Reading

Commercial films

This list is not intended to be complete. More films which include sequences shot in Reading can be found on the Reel Streets website (http://www.reelstreets.com).

The Stroke of the Phoebus Eight, 1913
Directed by Charles J. Brabin, starring Marc McDermott, Miriam Nesbitt and Charles Vernon, and produced by the Edison Company. The villain, the 'stroke' of a rowing crew who has become vain and self-satisfied, is replaced on the orders of the coach. The villain kidnaps his replacement, but the replacement manages to escape and take part in the race, which the crew win. Shot at Henley-on-Thames, using local people. It was shown at the Vaudeville in 1914.

The 39 Steps, 1935
A thriller directed by Alfred Hitchcock and starring Robert Donat and Madeleine Carroll. The plot is loosely based on the novel by John Buchan, though the episodes at the beginning and end involving 'Mr Memory' on the stage of a music hall theatre are pure Hitchcock. Most of the film was shot in Lime Grove Studios in London, but the theatre was a real one. Websites say that it was the London Palladium, but if you see the film, it is obvious that a smaller theatre was used. The *GetReading* website suggests it was the Palace Theatre in Cheapside, Reading. Unfortunately, photographs of the auditorium of the Palace seem to be non-existent, so it has not so far been possible to prove it.

Reach for the Sky, 1956

The story of the real Second World War airman Douglas Bader, played by Kenneth More in the film. It appears that none of the filming took place in Reading, and that Denham Aerodrome near Gerrard's Cross stood in for Woodley Aerodrome, Reading, from where Bader took off in 1931. As a result of the crash of the fateful flight, his legs had to be amputated at the Royal Berkshire Hospital, and though there are hospital scenes in the film, these were probably not filmed in Reading. In real life, Bader rejoined the RAF after the outbreak of war and became a national hero.

Lucky Jim, 1957

Based on the novel by Kingsley Amis and directed by John Boulting. This was a comedy about the escapades of a young lecturer at a red-brick university, with Ian Carmichael in the title role. Though the university wasn't Reading, there is a short sequence showing the Great Western Hotel (now the Malmaison) in Station Road, inside and out.

The Plank, 1967

Written by Eric Sykes, this was a 45-minute film shot in Caversham Park Village when it was under construction. It starred many famous comedy actors of the time, including Tommy Cooper, Jimmy Edwards and Sykes himself. The soundtrack was largely sound effects and grunts from the actors.

The Eagle Has Landed, 1976
Second World War drama about German troops invading an East Anglian village as part of a plot to capture Sir Winston Churchill, based on a novel by Jack Higgins, and starring Michael Caine and Donald Sutherland. Though strictly speaking not in Reading, the nearby church and watermill at Mapledurham were used. For the filming, several 'fake' buildings were added to the village, including a pub and a shop.

Bugsy Malone, 1976
A gangster movie set in New York in the Prohibition era, but with songs, and using child actors. It was made at Pinewood Studios at Iver Heath near Slough and used the Huntley and Palmers biscuit factory in King's Road, shortly before it was demolished, as the factory of Splurge Incorporated, which made the 'splurge guns' that fired something resembling custard.

A Bridge Too Far, 1976
Second World War epic starring Dirk Bogarde, James Caan, Michael Caine and Sean Connery. There is a scene in which locals watch aeroplanes flying overhead which was shot in Hill Street.

The Krays, 1990
Based on the career of the London gangsters Ronnie and Reggie Kray, and starring Martin and Gary Kemp. A fairground scene was shot in Prospect Park.

Let Him Have It, 1991
A film about the arrest and trial of Derek Bentley for murdering a policeman in 1952, when he was 16. Bentley was hanged, but the conviction was controversial. He received a partial posthumous pardon in 1993 and a complete pardon in 1998. Christopher Eccleston played Bentley in the film, which was made at Pinewood Studios. Exterior shots were around a house in Cranbury Road in west Reading which stood in for Bentley's 1950s home.

Cemetery Junction, 2010
An autobiographical comedy, written by and starring Ricky Gervais. Though based on his experiences growing up in Reading in the 1970s, the town wasn't used for location shots.

Burnt, 2015
American comedy drama starring Bradley Cooper as a chef who, in the end, gets his third Michelin star. The prison scenes were filmed at Reading.

Other films, including amateur films

The early film made in Reading in 1904 and showing workers coming out of the Huntley and Palmers factory has already been mentioned, as well as the likelihood of a film being made of the political meeting in the tram-sheds in 1910, at which David Lloyd-George was present. It would seem that there was also a film of the Reading Historical Pageant, which took place in the Abbey Ruins in June 1920. Among the contractors mentioned in the souvenir booklet, alongside the set builders, printers and bill posters, are Baron Hartlet Ltd., 'cinematograph film producers'. No print of any of these films is known to exist.

There are believed to be a couple of amateur films made about Reading in the 1960s, which it has not so far been possible to track down, but which informants remember having seen. Around 1960, there was a film called *All These People*, and in 1965, there was a film made by Doug Noyes entitled *Our Town*. Please get in touch with the History of Reading Society if you have information. Perhaps we will be able to see both of these films one day.

The official repository for old films for our area is the Wessex Film and Sound Archive, based at the Hampshire Record Office in Winchester. They have many films made in Reading, sometimes in colour, but usually in black and white, sometimes with a soundtrack, but often not. Many subjects are covered – such as royal visits, public information films on health issues, publicity films for Huntley and Palmers biscuits, and local trams and trolley-buses. Their website is at www3.hants.gov.uk/wfsa.

In addition to these commercial films, Reading has a society of amateur film makers: Reading Film and Video Makers. They can trace their origins back to 1953, when the Reading and District Cine Club began. After a few years, the name changed to Reading Tape Recording and Cine Society, bringing together sound and vision through audio tape, 35 mm slides and 8 mm cine film. In the 1980s, videotape arrived and, more recently, digital technology. The society can be contacted through their website, www.readingfilmandvideomakers.org.uk.

Of recent years, British Pathé and British Movietone News have made old cinema newsreels viewable on the internet. Search for films made in 'Reading, Berkshire' at www.britishPathé.com and www.aparchive.com.

Actors and directors with Reading connections

Ronald Allen, 1930-1991
Actor, born in Reading and educated at Leighton Park School. He did much stage work, and his films include 'A Night to Remember', about the sinking of the Titanic, but he is probably best remembered for the television soaps *Compact* and *Crossroads*.

Jacqueline Bisset, 1944-
Film actress. Grew up in Tilehurst, where her father was a general practitioner. She has made films in continental Europe, and in the United States, as well as in this country. They include *Airport*, *Bullitt*, *Casino Royale*, *Day for Night*, *The Deep*, and *Under the Volcano*.

The Boulting Brothers
Roy and John Boulting were twins, born in Bray in 1913. They were educated at Reading School, and were film producers and directors. Their films include *Brighton Rock*, *I'm Alright Jack*, *The Family Way*, and *Lucky Jim*.

Their elder brother, who took the name Peter Cotes, was an actor, writer and director in the theatre.

Sir Kenneth Branagh, 1960-
Actor and director. He was born in Belfast, and his family moved to Reading when he was nine years old. He was educated at The Grove Primary School and Whiteknights Primary School, and The Meadway Comprehensive School. He acted in school plays, with the Progress Theatre, and with

the Reading Cine and Video Society (now Reading Film and Video Makers). He has done much stage and television work, and acted in film versions of many Shakespeare plays. As a film director, he worked on *Mary Shelley's Frankenstein*, and *Sleuth*.

Robert Bridges, 1938–1988
Actor, born in Reading, the son of Oliver and Linda Bridges who ran the Reading Repertory Theatre. His sister, Sally, was an actress, and he was related by marriage to the Winslet family. Films include *Pink Floyd: The Wall*, *Morgan*, and *Footsteps*.

Jim Broadbent, 1949–
Actor. Went to Leighton Park School. Apart from much stage and television work, his films include *The Borrowers*, *The Iron Lady*, and *Topsy Turvy*.

Michael Carreras, 1927–1994
He was the son of James Carreras, the founder of Hammer Films, and was educated at Reading School. He worked for Hammer Studios as screenplay writer, producer, director and executive, and was involved with many films – including *The Curse of Frankenstein*, *Dracula*, *The Curse of the Werewolf*, and *The Curse of the Mummy's Tomb*.

Lisa Daniely, 1929–2014
Film and television actress born Mary Elizabeth Bodington in Reading, where her father was a solicitor. Her mother was French, and she was educated in Paris. Her films include *Lili Marlene*, *Hindle Wakes*, and *Tiger by the Tail*.

Natalie Dormer, 1982–
Film and television actress, born in Reading, and educated at Chiltern Edge School at Sonning Common, and in the sixth form at Reading Blue Coat School. Whilst as school, she attended the Allenova School of Dancing. She is well known for her television work, but has appeared in films, including *Casanova*, *W.E.*, and *Captain America: The First Avenger*.

Winston Ellis, 1965–
Film and television actor, film producer and martial arts champion. Born in Reading, to Jamaican parents. Films include *Pirates of the Caribbean: Dead Man's Chest*, and *Pirates of the Caribbean: At World's End*.

Lilian Fontaine, 1886–1975
Film and television actress born in Reading, Lilian Augusta Ruse. As a girl, she lived in Zinzan Street. After a stage career in England, she married Walter Augustus de Havilland in New York in 1914, and they had two daughters, Olivia and Joan, born in 1916 and 1917 respectively. In 1925, Lilian and Walter divorced, and she married George Fontaine. Her daughters were both film stars, Olivia de Havilland and Joan Fontaine. Lilian starred in several films in the 1940s and 1950s, including *The Lost Weekend* and *The Bigamist*.

Ricky Gervais, 1961–
Actor, writer, comedian. Born in Battle Hospital, and was brought up in the Whitley area. He attended Whitley Park Infants' and Junior Schools, and Ashmead Comprehensive School, before going to London University to take a degree in philosophy. He had a career in music and radio, before his big television break-through, *The Office*. He had roles in films such as *Ghost Town* and *The Invention of Lying*, before the film he co-wrote and starred in, *Cemetery Junction*.

Arthur Hambling, 1888–1952
Actor; he was the son of architect W.G.A. Hambling of Reading, and was himself an architect before becoming an actor. He appeared in over 40 films from the 1930s to the 1950s, including *King Henry V*, and *The Lavender Hill Mob*.

Stacy Keach, 1941–
American actor and narrator, in films, on television and on stage. He is remembered in Reading for being arrested at Heathrow airport in 1984 for possession of cocaine, and being tried at Reading Crown Court, where he pleaded guilty. He was imprisoned in Reading Gaol for six months.

David Lean, CBE, 1908–1991
Film director, educated at Leighton Park School. Films include *The Bridge on the River Kwai*, *Brief Encounter*, *Dr. Zhivago*, *Great Expectations*, *Lawrence of Arabia*, and *Oliver Twist*.

Francesca Longrigg, 1961–
Film and television actress and writer, born in Reading. Her films include *Empire of the Sun*, *Pirate Radio*, and *Star Wars: The Force Awakens*.

Cherith Mellor, 1946–
Actress, born in Reading in 1946. She has done much television work; films include *Mrs. Brown*, *Sam* and *Some Kind of Life*.

Sam Mendes, CBE, 1965–
Stage and film director. He was born in Reading where his father was a university lecturer, but his parents divorced whilst he was a child, and most of his upbringing was in Oxfordshire.

His film credits include *American Beauty*, the two James Bond films *Skyfall* and *Spectre*, and the film versions of the stage musicals *Cabaret* and *Oliver*. He was married to actress Kate Winslet between 2003 and 2011. They were both born in Reading.

Alana Morshead, 1983–
Actress, film director and costume designer, born in Reading. Films include *Joe Millionaire*, *The Story of Elle*, and *Equals*.

Peter Reeves, 1932–
Actor, born in Reading. His films include *What a Girl Wants*, *Love Among the Ruins*, and *Dick Deadeye, or Duty Done*.

Peter Shaw, 1918–2003
Born Peter Pullen in Reading, and worked in Hollywood, as a film actor, producer and studio executive. He was married to actress Angela Lansbury.

Jason Stevens, 1973–
Actor, born in Reading. Films include *Lost Dogs* and *The Kindness of Strangers*.

Peter Strickland, 1973–
Film director and screen writer, born in Reading, where is parents were teachers. He went to Reading Bluecoat School, and acted with Progress Theatre. He has won awards at international film festivals, and his films include *Katalin Varga*, *Berberian Sound Studio*, and *The Duke of Burgundy*.

Victoria Summer, 1981–

Actress, model, singer and songwriter. She was born in Reading, and her first screen role was in *The Zombie Diaries*, a low-budget horror film. She subsequently moved to Los Angeles, where her films were *Dracula Reborn*, *How Sweet it Is*, *Saving Mr Banks*, and *Game of Aces*.

Kate Winslet, CBE, 1975–

Film actress. Born and brought up in Reading, she appeared in many of the productions of the Starmaker Theatre Company, and went on to study at the Redroofs Theatre School at Littlewick Green, near Maidenhead. Her father, Roger, married Olive Bridges, the sister of Robert Bridges, the actor, and Roger Bridges is himself an actor and musician. Kate's sisters, Anna and Beth, are both accomplished actresses. Kate's films include *The Dressmaker*, *Finding Neverland*, *Hamlet*, *Iris*, *Jude*, *Steve Jobs*, and *Titanic*. She was married to stage and film director Sam Mendes between 2003 and 2011: he had also been born in Reading.

Ken Wynne, 1920–2012

Television and film actor, born in Reading, Ken Wynne. He did a lot of television work: films include *Up Pompeii* and *Up the Chastity Belt*.

Ownership of cinemas in Reading

Cinema	Owner where known

King's Hall, 1909–c.1915
  Bio-Picture Land (1909–1910)
  Standard Electric Theatre (1910–1915)
	Standard Electric Theatres

Vaudeville Electric Theatre, 1909–1957 Gaumont (1953–1957)	White family (1909–1929) County Cinemas (1929–1937) Odeon Cinemas (1937–1941) J. Arthur Rank (1941–1957)
West's Picture Palace, 1909–c.1916	T.J. West
Electric Automatic Vaudeville, 1910	
Empire Picture Theatre, 1911–c.1930	C.J. Stanley (1920–1930)
Caversham Electric Theatre, 1911–1977 Glendale (1945–1977)	C.J. Stanley (1920–1977)
Paragon Electric Theatre, 1911–c.1913	J.A. Lowe & G. Baker
Howard Electric Theatre, 1911–c.1913	W.H. Dee
Grand, 1911–1922	W. Vincent & E. Reed
London Street Pavilion, 1920–?	
Tilehurst Cinema, 1920–c.1929	

Central Picture Playhouse, 1921–1999
  ABC Central (1943–1986)
  Cannon (1986–1994)
  MGM (1994–1999)
	ABC (1935–1986)
	Cannon (1986–1994)
	MGM (1994–1999)

Pavilion, 1929–1979 Gaumont (1957–1979)	Fort family (1929–1930) County Cinemas (1930) Odeon Cinemas (1937–1941) J. Arthur Rank (1941–1979)

Granby, 1935–1982
  ABC Granby (1943–1979)
  ABC London Road (1979–1982)
	Simmons Theatres (1935–1941)
	Mayfair Cinemas (1941–1943)
	ABC (1943–1982)

Savoy, 1936–1961	Simmons Theatres (1936–1943) ABC (1943–1961)
Odeon, 1937–1999	Odeon Cinemas (1937–1941) ABC (1941–1999)
Rex, 1937–1958	Simmons Theatres (1937–1943) ABC (1943–1958)
Regal, 1938–1958	Simmons Theatres (1938–1943) ABC (1943–1958)
Reading Film Theatre, 1970–	
Studios 1 and 2, 1972–1978	Star Group
Warner Village, 1999– Vue (2004–)	Warner Brothers (1999–2003) SPC (2003–)
Showcase, 1996–	National Amusements (UK) Ltd.

Sources

Most of the information in this book comes from the local newspapers in Reading Central Library. Besides microfilm copies of all of the papers, there is a collection of newspaper cuttings on cinemas that has proved invaluable. Other sources are listed below.

Cinema Theatre Association Bulletin, vol. 13 No. 4, July–August 1979. [This is largely a reprint of an article by Leslie North, 'Animated Pictures Aided Soup Kitchen', which was published in the *Reading Chronicle* on 17 November 1958.] There is a copy in Reading Central Library.

Cinema Theatre Association. Reading and Wokingham. Sunday 21 June 1987. [Itinerary for a visit to cinemas in Reading and Wokingham, with notes on the buildings to be visited.] There is a copy in Reading Central Library.

Goad plans. A series of large-scale plans of Reading town centre, showing commercial premises, produced by Charles E. Goad and Company. The 1913 edition is particularly useful for showing the exact locations of the early cinemas. There are copies of the maps in the Central Library.

Gold, Sidney M., *A Biographical Dictionary of Architects at Reading*. Reading: privately published, 1999.

Granby Cinema, Souvenir programme of the opening, 1935. Berkshire Record Office T/A 85.

Hylton, Stuart, *Reading: the 1950s*. Second edition. Stroud: The History Press, 2013.

Owen, Wilfred, *Wilfred Owen. Collected Letters*, edited by Harold Owen and John Bell. London: Oxford University Press, 1967, p. 162.

Phillips, Daphne J. *Reading Theatres, Cinemas and Other Entertainments, 1788–1978*. Reading: Reading Libraries, 1978.

Reading Borough Council committee minutes record the granting and renewal of licences for cinemas under the 1909 Cinematograph Act, and can be seen at Reading Central Library and the Berkshire Record Office.

Souvenir of the Reading Historical Pageant, held in the Abbey Ruins, June 21st–26th 1920. Reading: The Pageant Committee, 1920.

Shaw, Richard, *Heritage Open Days, 1995*. [Notes on the history of the MGM Cinema, formerly the Central Cinema, ABC Cinema and Cannon Cinema, prepared for a Heritage Open Days tour by the manager]

Vaudeville Cinema. Illustrated Synopsis of the film *Queen Bess*, 1912. Berkshire Record Office DEX 534/3.

Vaudeville Cinema. Pamphlet giving notice of forthcoming attractions, November 1922. Berkshire Record Office DEX 572/3.

Woodeson, William Edward, *Memories, Observations and Gleanings of Reading Town*. Unpublished typescript, 1967. There is a copy at Reading Central Library.

www.cinematreasures.org. Contains photographs of a number of cinemas in Reading.

www.getreading.co.uk. An internet search under 'film locations reading' brought up a useful list on the GetReading website, August 2016.

www.historicengland.org.uk. Its archive contains a splendid set of photographs of the Odeon, Reading.

www.reelstreets.com. This website can be searched to find films containing sequences shot in Reading – or any other place in the country.

Index

References in bold type indicate a major entry. The occasional reference in italics indicates a picture.

3-D   **7**, 30
70mm film   7, 8
A.H. Bull's   10, 34, 38
ABC Central   8, 15, 20, 23, 30, 31, **63**, 69. *See also* Central Cinema, Cannon, MGM
ABC cinema chain   17, 18, 29, 61, 68, 72, 78, 80
ABC Granby   7, **66–69**. *See also* Granby; ABC London Road
ABC London Road   69. *See also* Granby; ABC Granby
ABC minors   23, 61
actors   91–96
  Bisset, Jacqueline   91
  Branagh, Kenneth   91
  Broadbent, Jim   92
  Gervais, Ricky   93
  Winslet, Kate   96
  Zettering, Mai   81
admission prices   **14–5**, 34, 36, 54, 56, 79
amateur film   89–90
architects
  Bailey, Eric Norman   17, 70, 76, 79
  Emden, Egan and Company   40
  Gardiner, George   59
  Matcham, Frank   47
  Ravenscroft, Ernest   50
  Scott, Harold S.   63
  Simmons, Edgar   17, 66
  Sprague, W.G.R.   35
  Starkey, A. Percival   72
  Webb, G.W.   56

Arnold's Electric Bioscope   11, *33*
Associated British Picture Corporation *see* ABC Cinema chain
audiences   30–1, 54, 61

bars, licensed   7, 27, 68, 85
Bio-Picture Land *see* King's Hall
bioscopes   5, 11, 14, 32–33
British Board of Film Censors   19
British Board of Film Classification   19
British Film Institute   18, 81
British Movietone News   77, 90
British Pathé   90

cafés   27, 40, 61, 67
Cannon, The   63. *See also* Central Cinema, ABC Central, MGM
Cannon Cinemas Group   29, 61, 63
Caversham Court Gardens   85
Caversham Electric [Theatre]   12, 14, 16, 18, **50–53**. *See also* Glendale
censorship   19–20
Central Cinema   6, 12, 26, **59–63**. *See also* ABC Central, Cannon, MGM
Central Picture Playhouse   *see* Central Cinema
children   37, 51, 61
children's programmes   22–24, 36, 37, 61
cinema owners   *see* ownership
cinemas   *see under names of individual cinemas*
CinemaScope   6, 8
cinematograph   10, 18, 32, 33, 34, 46, 37, 44
Cinematograph Act, 1909   11
Cinematograph Fund   18
Cinematographic Film Act, 1927   22
Cinerama   8
colour   4–5, 7, 56
County Cinemas   18, 43, 65

digital projection   8–9
directors
　Boulting Brothers   91
　Branagh, Kenneth   91–2
　Lean, David   94
　Mendes, Sam   84
　Morshead, Alana   95
　Strickland, Peter   95

Electric Supply Company   4
Electric Automatic Vaudeville   20, 36, **47–48**, 56
Electric Vaudeville   *see* Vaudeville Electric Theatre
Electrical and Musical Industries (EMI)   61
electricity   4
Empire Picture Theatre   12, 16, 24, **49–50**, 51
Entertainment Tax   14

fairs   2, 10, 14, 32
film   3–4
films
　A Bridge Too Far   88
　Bugsy Malone   88
　Burnt   89
　Cemetery Junction   89
　Eagle Has Landed, The   88
　Furthest South with Lieutenant Shackleton and the British Antarctic Expedition   42
　House of Wax   7
　In the Shadow of the Throne   42
　Krays, The   88
　Last Temptation of Christ, The   20
　Let Him Have It   89
　Little Dorrit   83
　Lucky Jim   87

Marriage Forbidden 19
Peeping Tom 19
Plank, The 87
Psycho 20
Pygmalion 4
Queen Bess 4, 20
Reach for the Sky 87
Rock Around the Clock 19
Scenery in Norway 4
Showboat 63
Stroke of the Phoebus Eight, The 42, 86
39 Steps, The 86
Weary River 6
fire 11–12, 78
Forbury Hotel 85
Fox Talbot, W.H. 2

Gaumont, Leon 3, 44
Gaumont-British Picture Corporation 44
Gaumont Cinema (Broad Street) 7, 43–44. *See also* Vaudeville Electric Theatre
Gaumont Cinema (Oxford Road) 63–5. *See also* Pavilion
ghost shows 2
Glendale 30, 31, 50–54. *See also* Caversham Electric Theatre
Glendale Theatres Corporation 53
Granby, The 8, 12, 14, 17, 23, 27, 30, 63, 66–69
Granby Cinema Company 17, 66
Grand, The 5, 12, 14, 16, 26, 56–7

Hexagon, The 83
Howard Cinema see Howard Electric Theatre
Howard Electric Theatre 12, 16, 36, 55
Huntley and Palmers 10, 15, 88, 90

I-Max® cinemas 8

105

J. Arthur Rank Organisation *see* Rank Organisation

Kinemacolor   5, 56
Kinetophone   6
King's Hall   3, 4, 12, 14, 22, 27, 32, **36–8**

legislation
  Cinematograph Act, 1909   11
  Cinematographic Film Act, 1927   22
  Sunday Entertainments Act, 1932   18
licensing   11, 12, 13, 34, 54, 56, 58, 83
live streaming   9, 31
locations, filming
  Caversham Park Village   87
  Cranbury Road, Reading   89
  Great Western Hotel   87
  Henley-on-Thames   86
  Hill Street, Reading   88
  Huntley and Palmers   88
  Mapledurham   88
  Prospect Park   88
  Reading Gaol   89
London Street Pavilion   **58**
Lumière Brothers   3, 10

MGM, The (cinema)   15, 30, 63. *See also* Central cinema, ABC Central, Cannon
Managers
  Bode, Milton   17, 47
  Crossley, Fred   61
  Fort, R.F.   63
  Hemming, Henry Charles   55
  Simmons, Mollie (Mrs Walter)   17, 66, 67
  Simmons Walter   17

Smith, F.W. Ogden   36, 37
Turner, Hermon   56
Marquis of Granby   69
Mayfair Cinemas   17, 68
Metro-Goldwyn Meyer   63
Mickey Mouse Club   23–4
Morley, H.T. (Tom)   32
multiplexes   7, 8, 15. *See also* Vue, Showcase, Warner Village
music   5, 6, 21, 24–26, 36, 42, 43, 46, 61, 63, 74
music hall   39

New Century Pictures   34

Odeon, The   12, 15, 17–8, 23–4, 30, 35, **72–76**
Odeon Cinemas   43, 65
Odeon Children's Club   24
Oracle shopping centre   15, 83
orchestras   5, 21, 24–6, 42, 46, 60
organs   26, 43, 63, 65
outdoor cinema   85
Owen, Wilfred   3–4, 46
ownership   16–18, 97–8. *See also* individual companies

Palace Bioscope   35
Palace Theatre   11, 17, **35**, 74, 86
Palace Theatre Company   17
Paragon Electric Theatre   4, 12, 16, **54–5**
Pathé, British   90
Pathé Brothers   3, 21–2, 42
Pathé Cinematograph Company   34
Pavilion (London Street)   *see* London Street Pavilion
Pavilion (Oxford Road)   6, 12, 14, 16, 18, 26, 27, 44, **63–5**.
   See also Gaumont
Penny Plunge   22, 37, 49

photography   2–3
pianos   5, 24, 26, 36
Poole's Myriorama   34
Prescott, Gerry   76
programmes   20–24
projectors   2, 5, 6, 8, 11, 41, 50, 56

Rank Organisation   18, 44, 65, 72, 76
Reading Film Society   81
Reading Film Theatre   30, 63, 81
Reading Picture Palace   12, **35–6**
Reading Town Halls   10, 13, **33–4**, 42, 83
Regal, The   12, 14, 17, 23, 54, **79–80**
Rex, The   7, 12, 14, 17, 18, 23, 30, **76–78**
Royal County Theatre   11, 17, **47**

safety   11–12
Savoy, The   12, 14, 17, 18, **70–72**
SBC International Cinemas   84
screens   2, 7–8, 44, 67, 68, 74, 84
Showcase   15
Simmons family   16–17, 66
Simmons Theatres   16–17, 66, 70, 76, 79
Smith, Roy   30
smoking   29
sound   5–7, 8, 22, 26, 60, 67, 68
soundtracks   6, 7
Standard Electric Theatre   *see* King's Hall
Star Group   82
stereophonic sound   6–7
Studios 1 and 2   15, **82**
Sunday Entertainments Act, 1932   18
Sunday opening   14, **18**, 37

talking pictures   6, 26, 60, 63, 74
Technicolor   5
Theatres Licensing Committee   19, 36
ticket prices   14-5, 34, 36, 54, 56, 79
Tilehurst Cinema   58-9
travelling shows   10-11, 32-3, 34

vaudeville   39
Vaudeville Electric Theatre   **38-44**. *See also* Gaumont
Vue   31, 84. *See also* Warner Village

Warner Village   15, 76, **83-4**. *See also* Vue
Watch Committee   12, 18, 19
West, Thomas James   44-5
West's Picture Palace   5, 12, 14, 16, 22, 24, **44-7**
wide screens   7-8

Two Rivers Press has been publishing in and
about Reading since 1994. Founded by the artist
Peter Hay (1951–2003), the press continues to delight
readers, local and further afield, with its varied list
of individually designed, thought-provoking books.